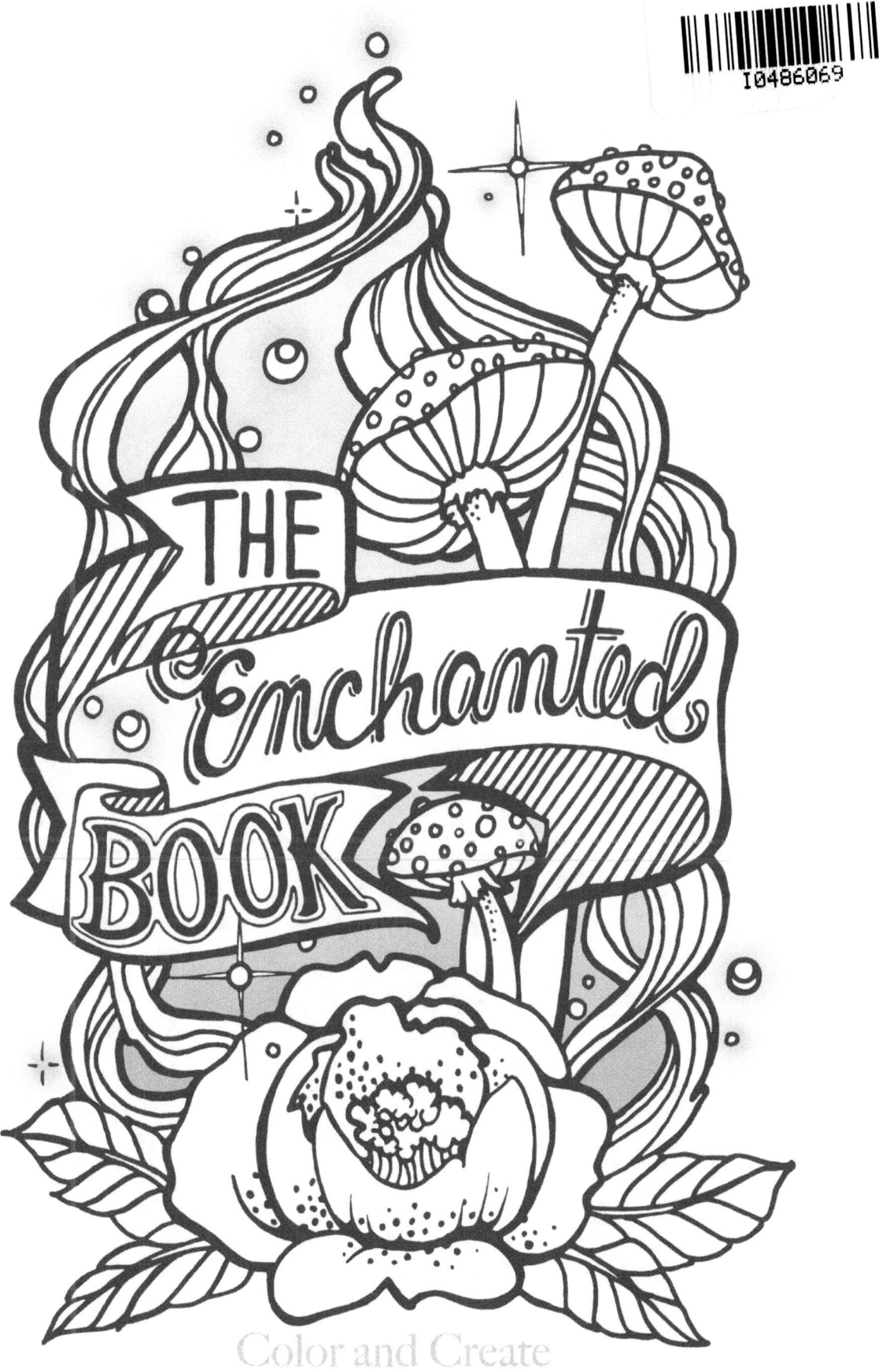

THE Enchanted BOOK

Color and Create

Jamie Lynn Dougherty

THE ENCHANTED BOOK

By Jamie Lynn Dougherty

www.jamiedoughertydesigns.com
email: info@jamiedoughertydesigns.com

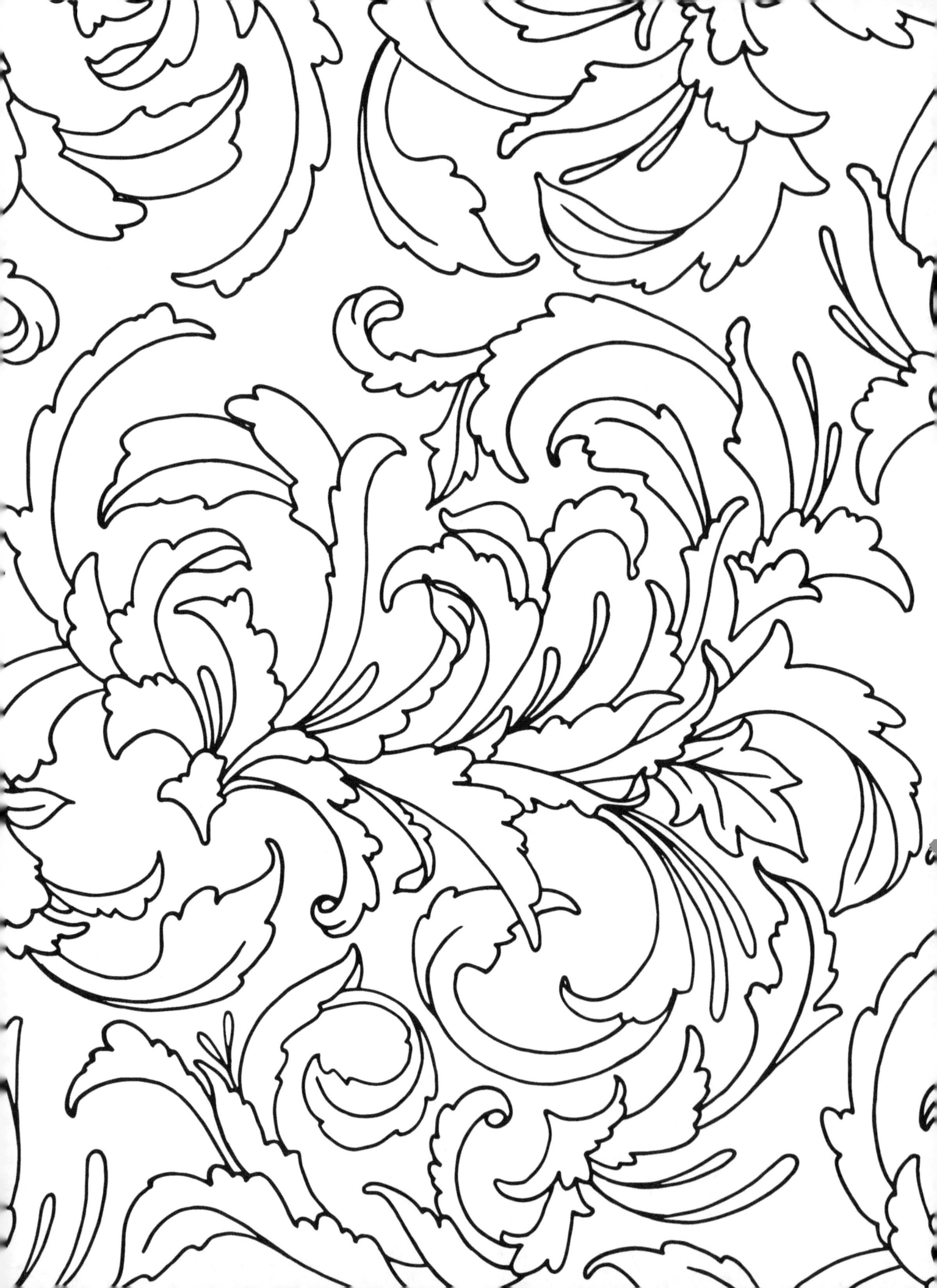

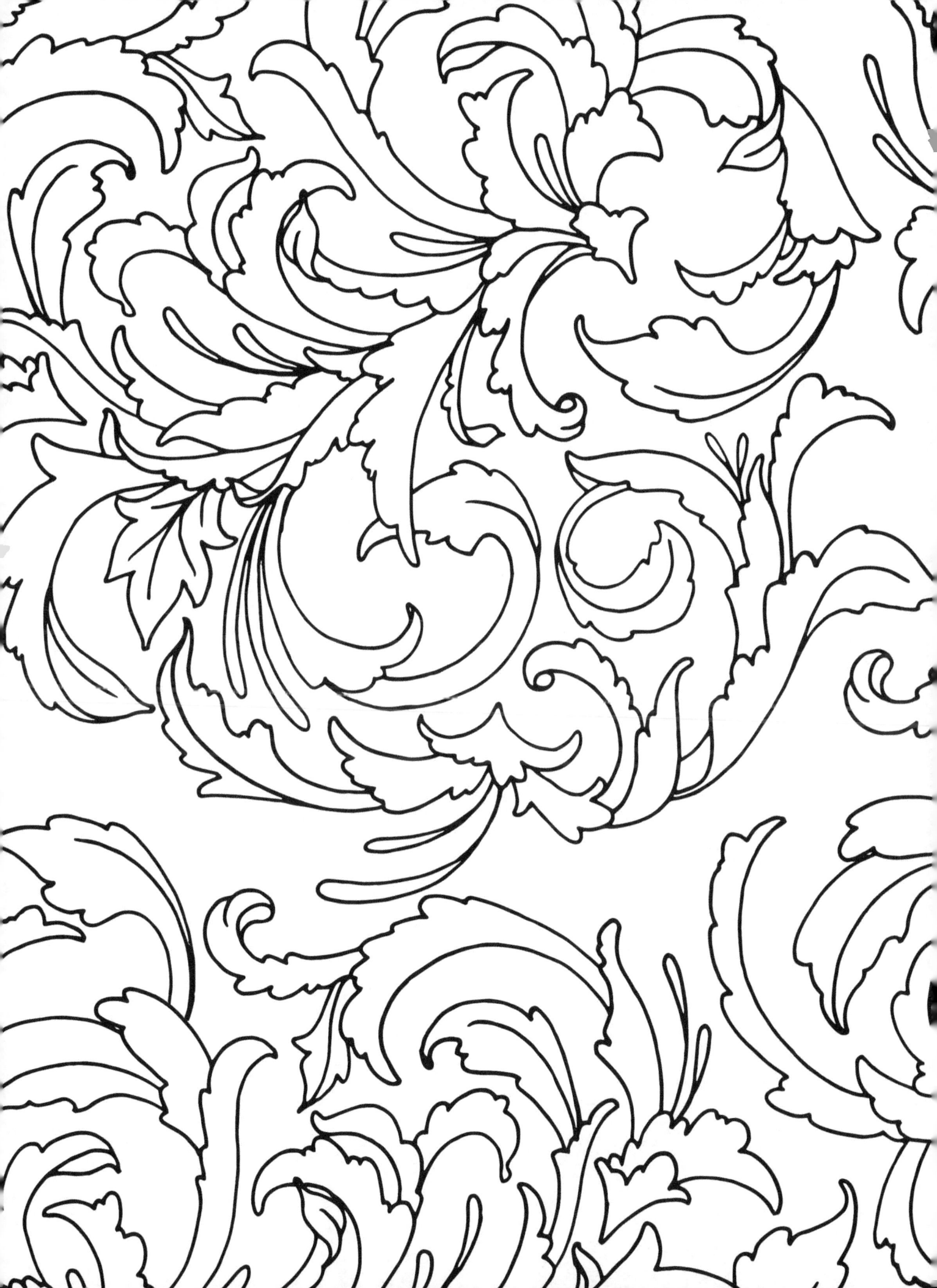

Beauty and the Beast

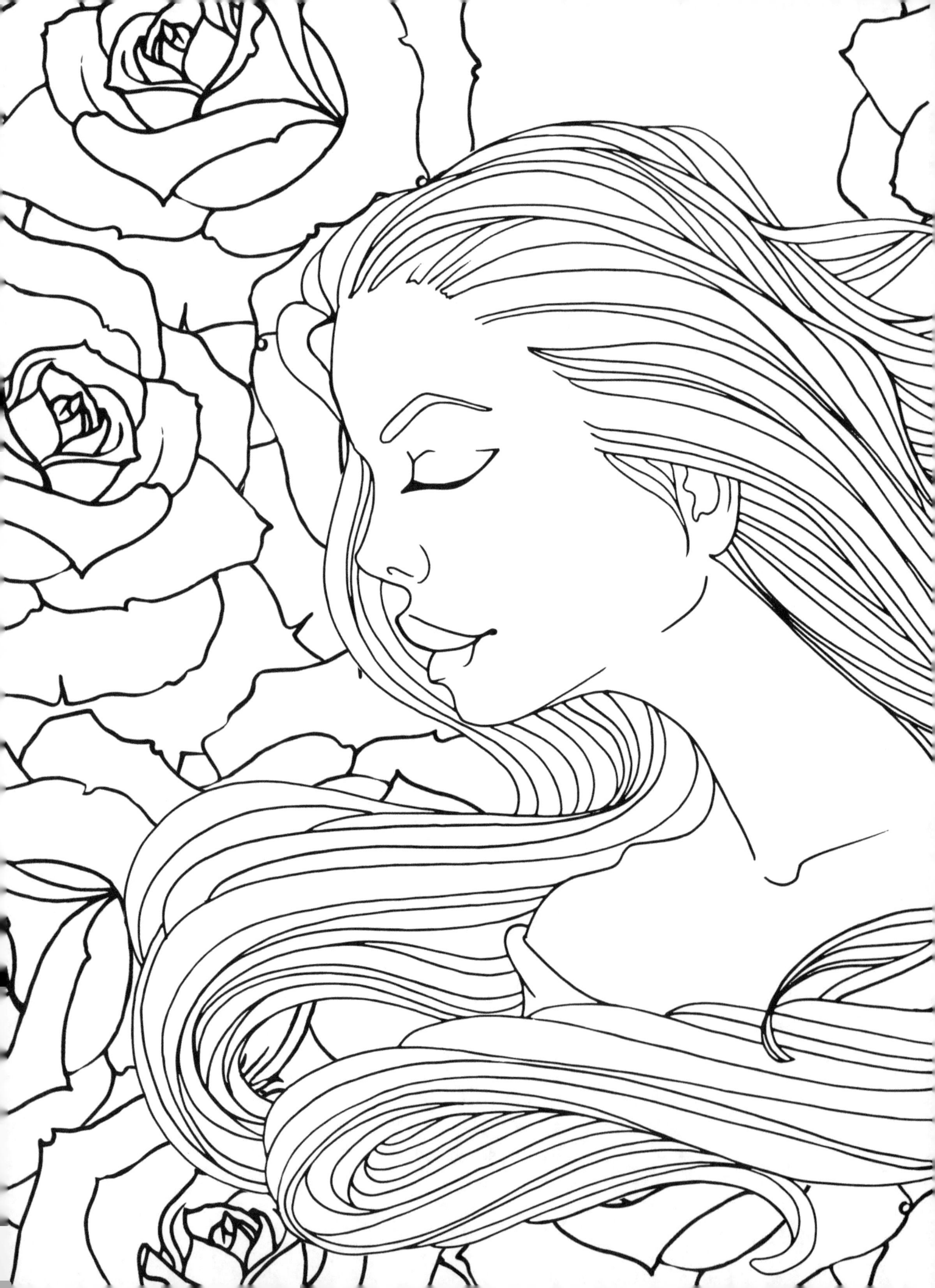

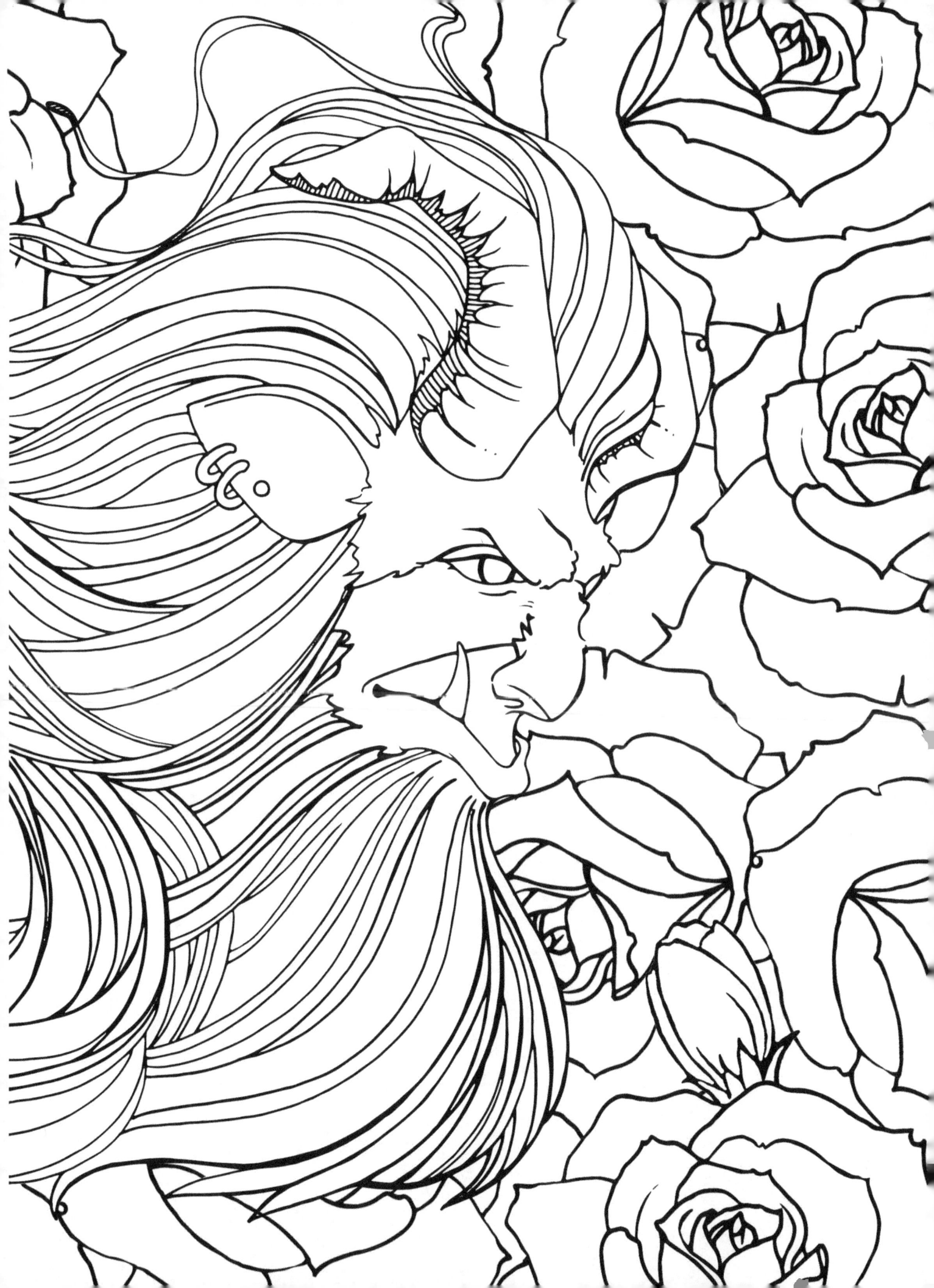

The One White Bride One Black Bride

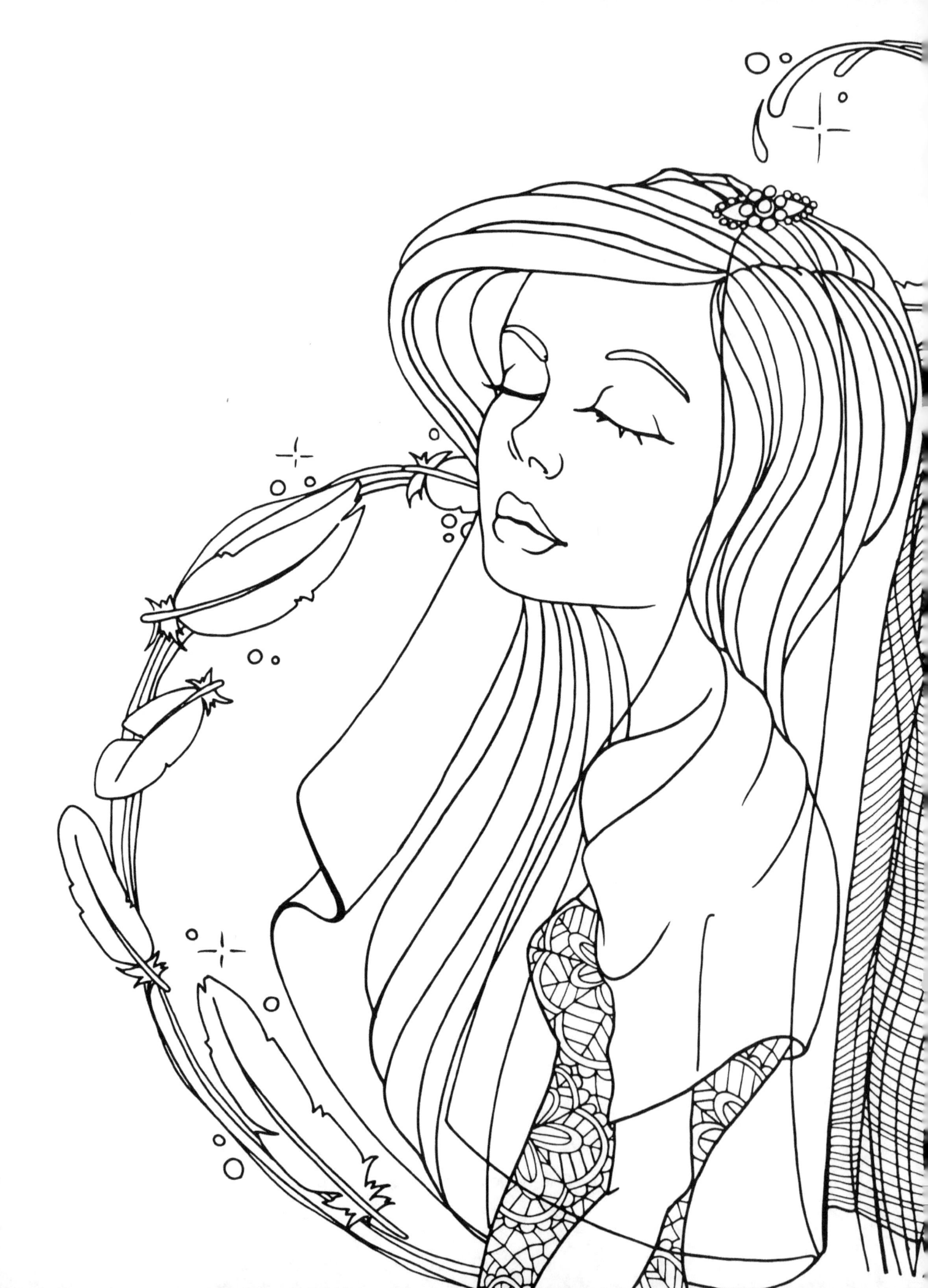

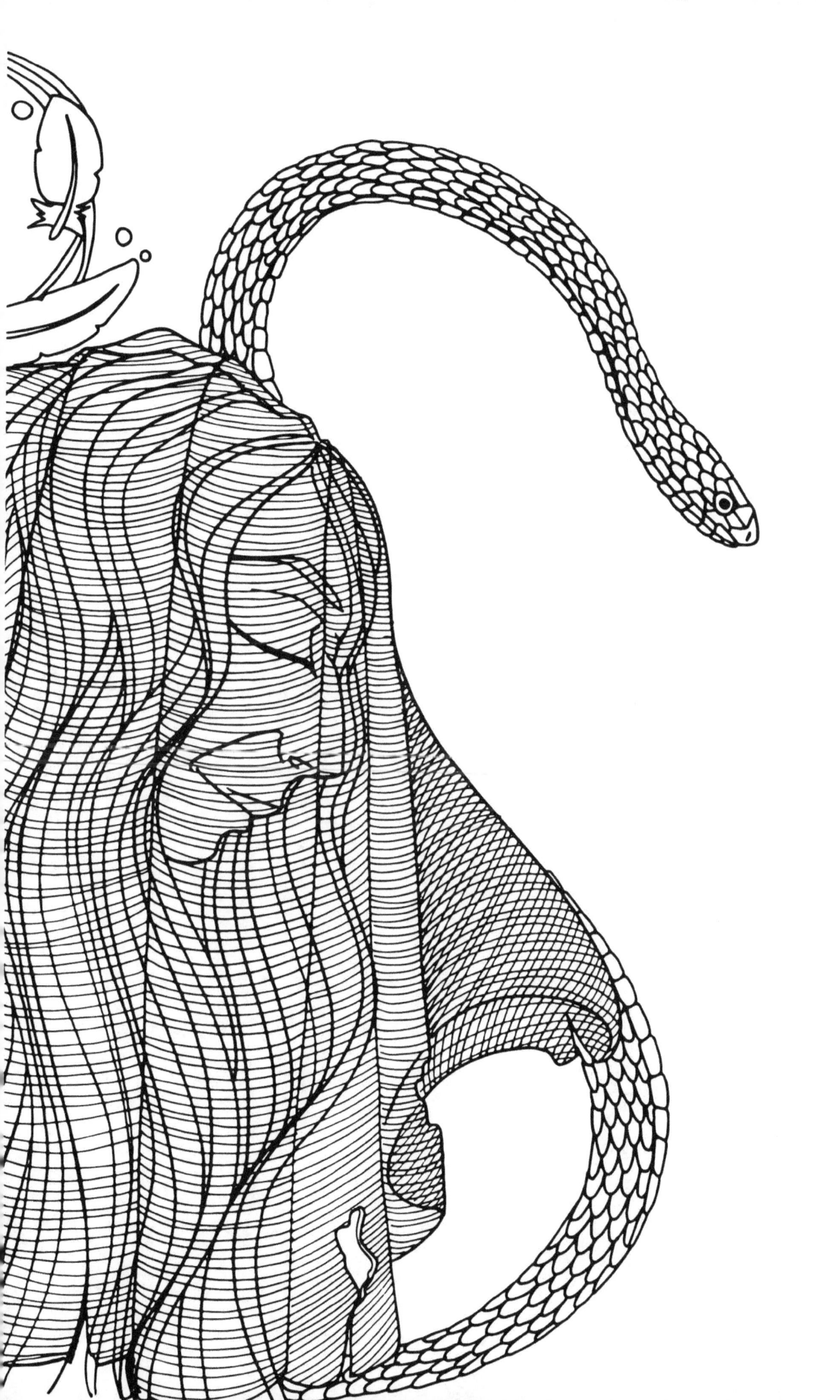

Little Red Riding Hood

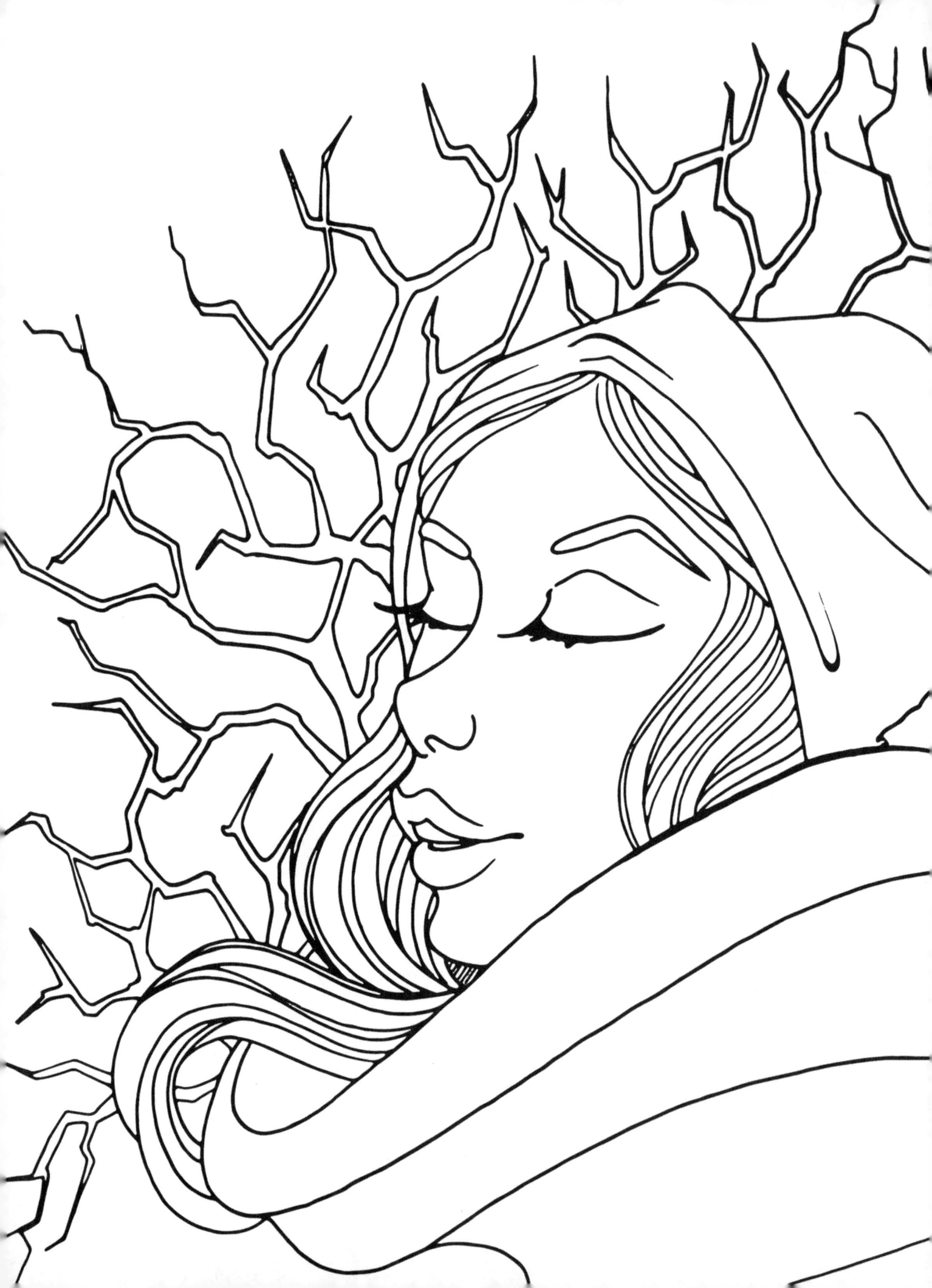

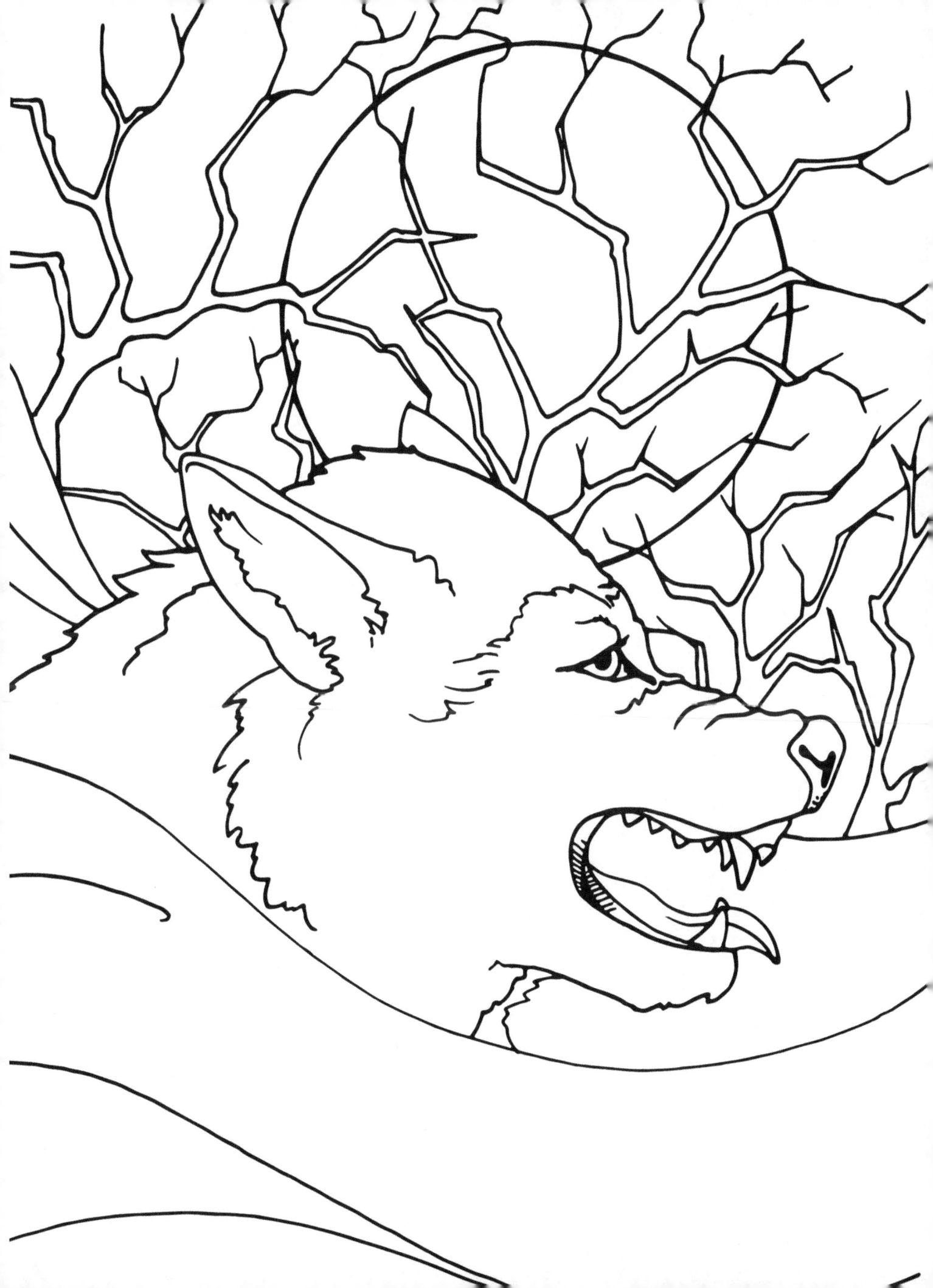

Alice In Wonderland

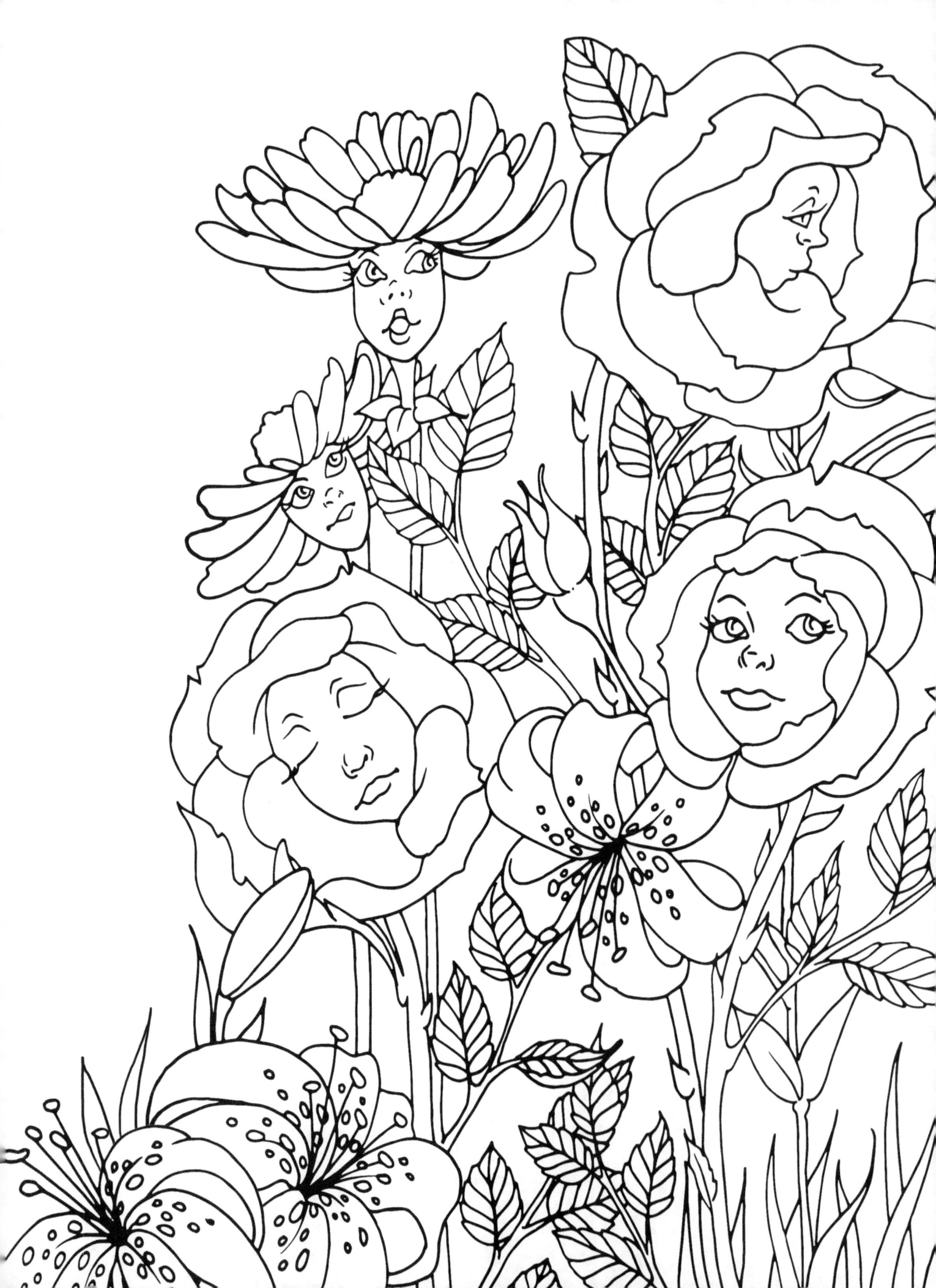

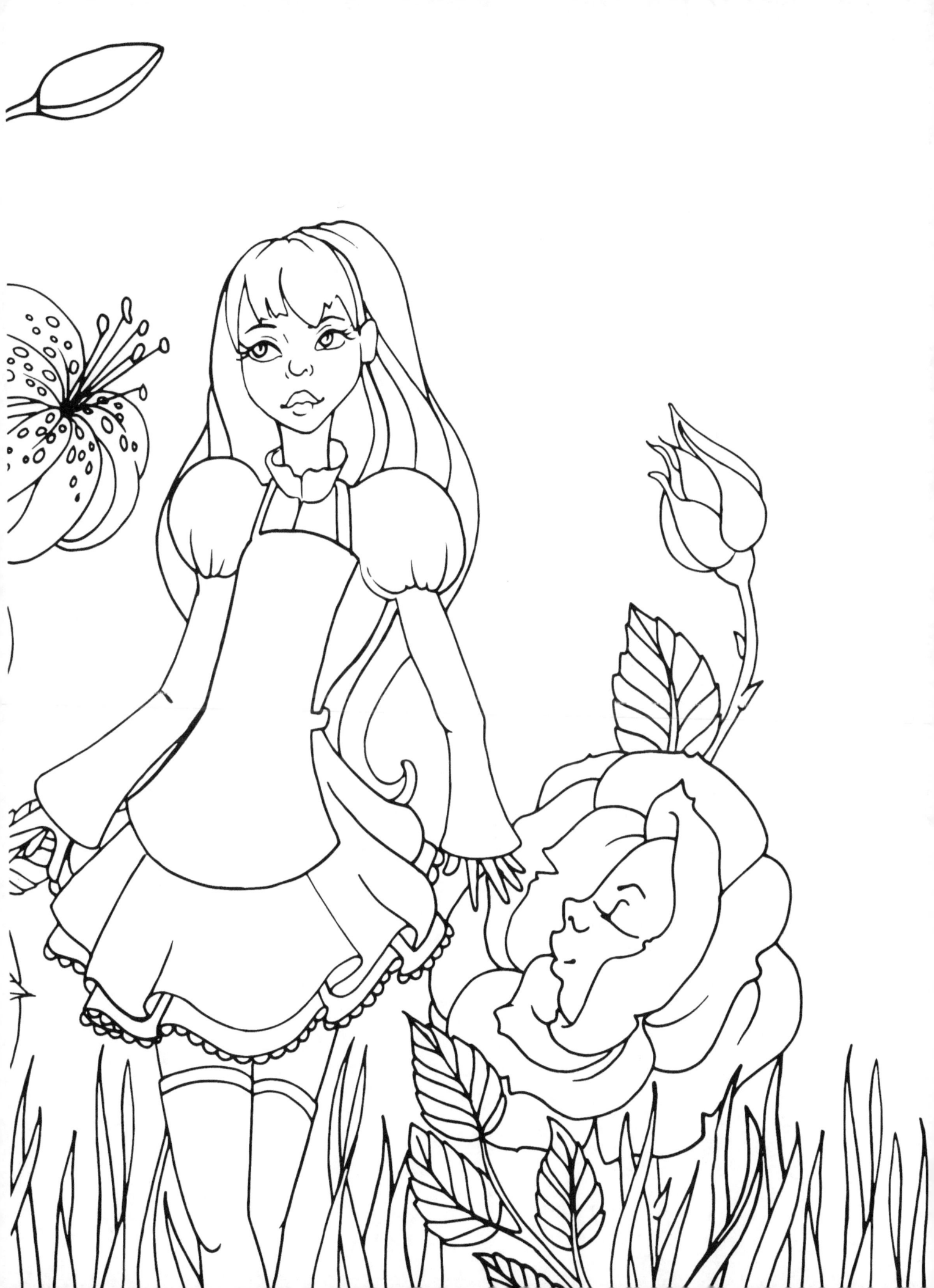

Thumbelina's Slumber

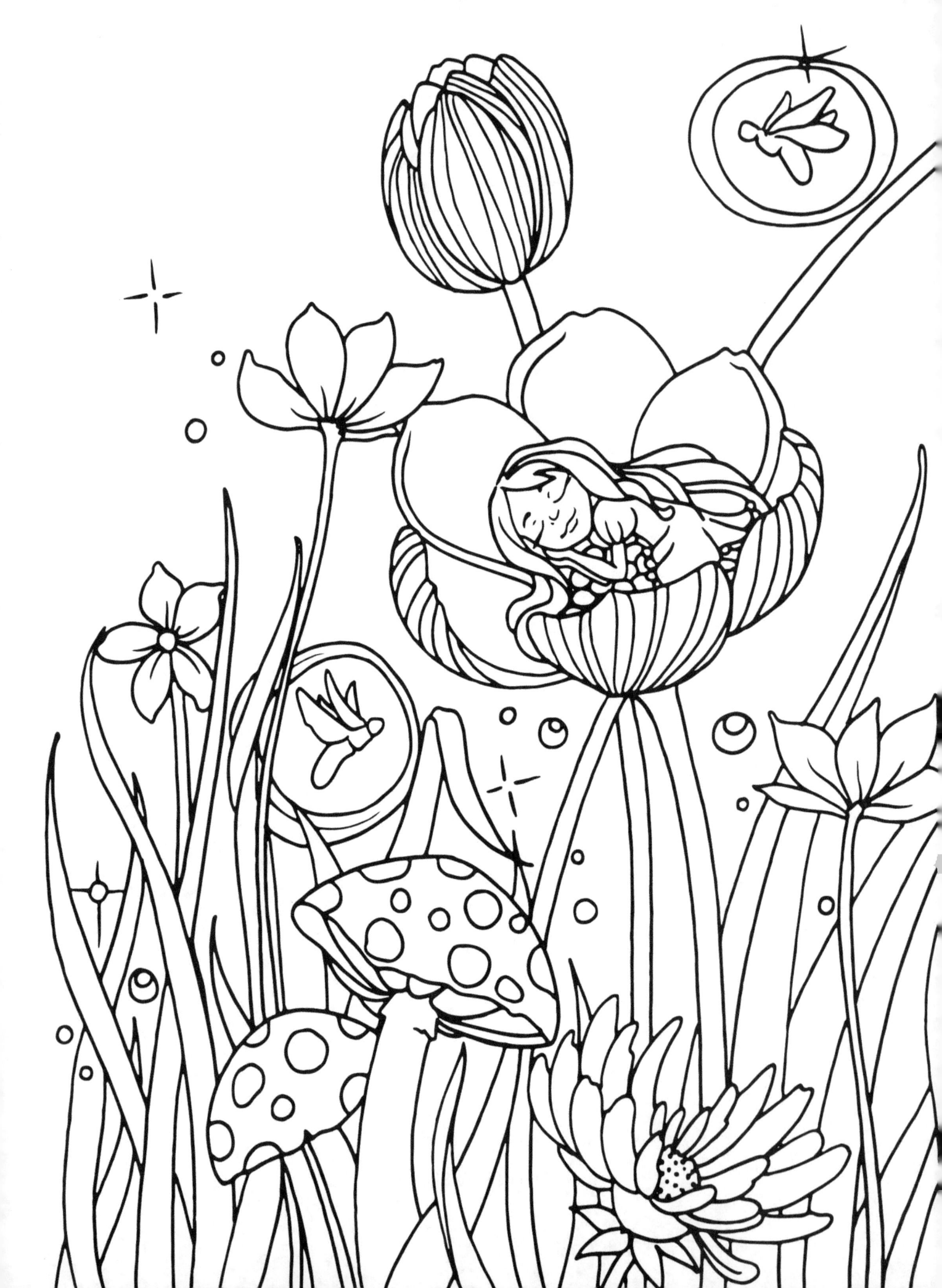

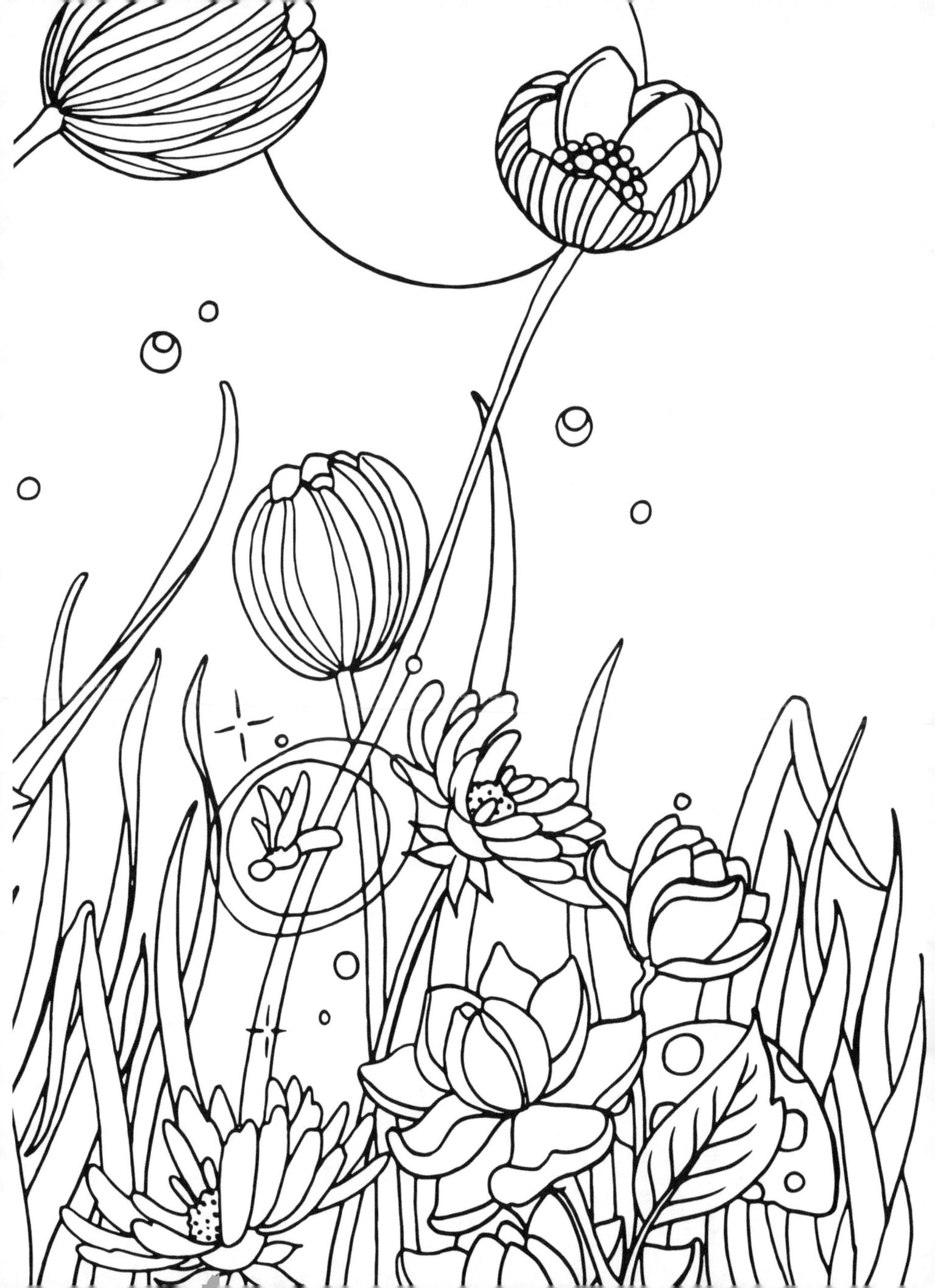

The Apple
Snow White

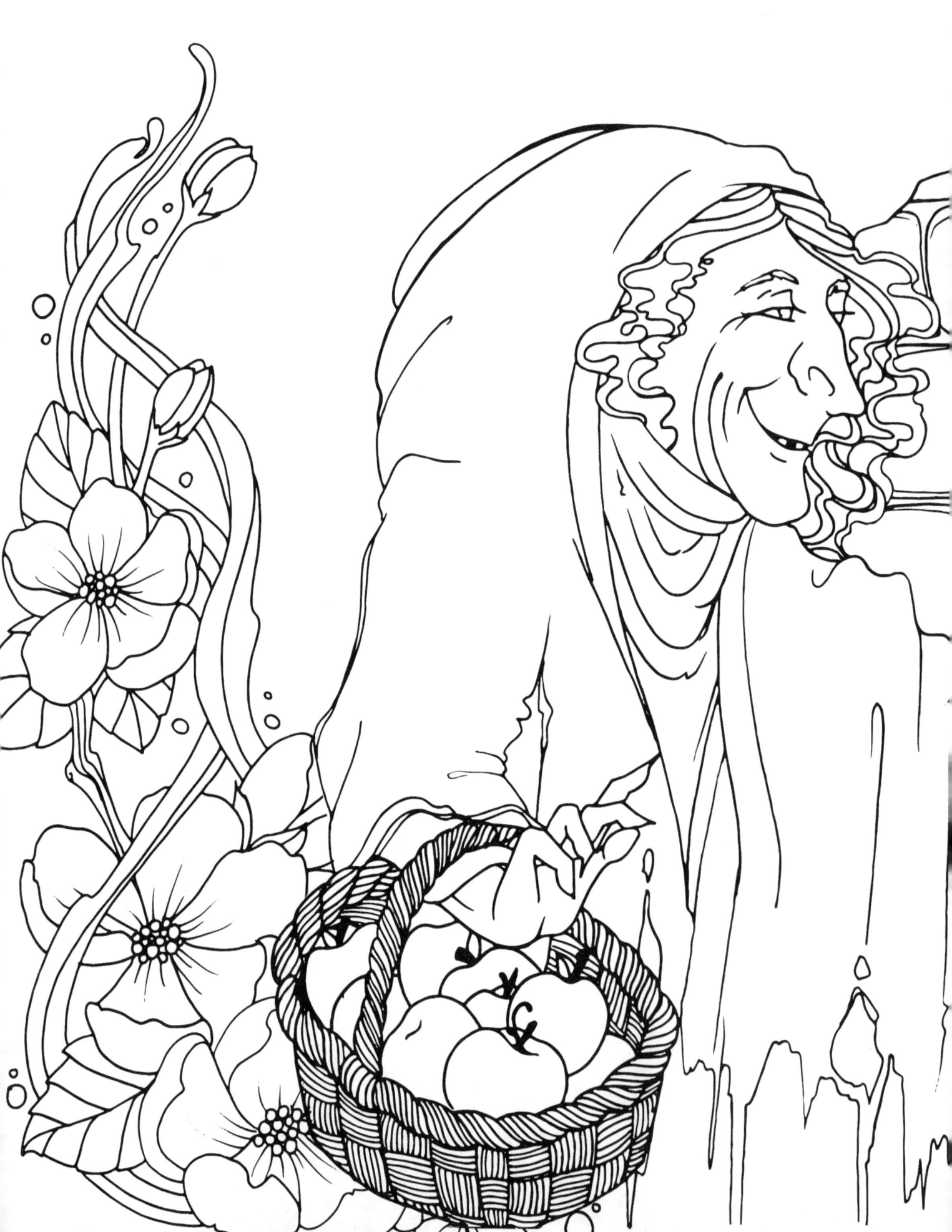

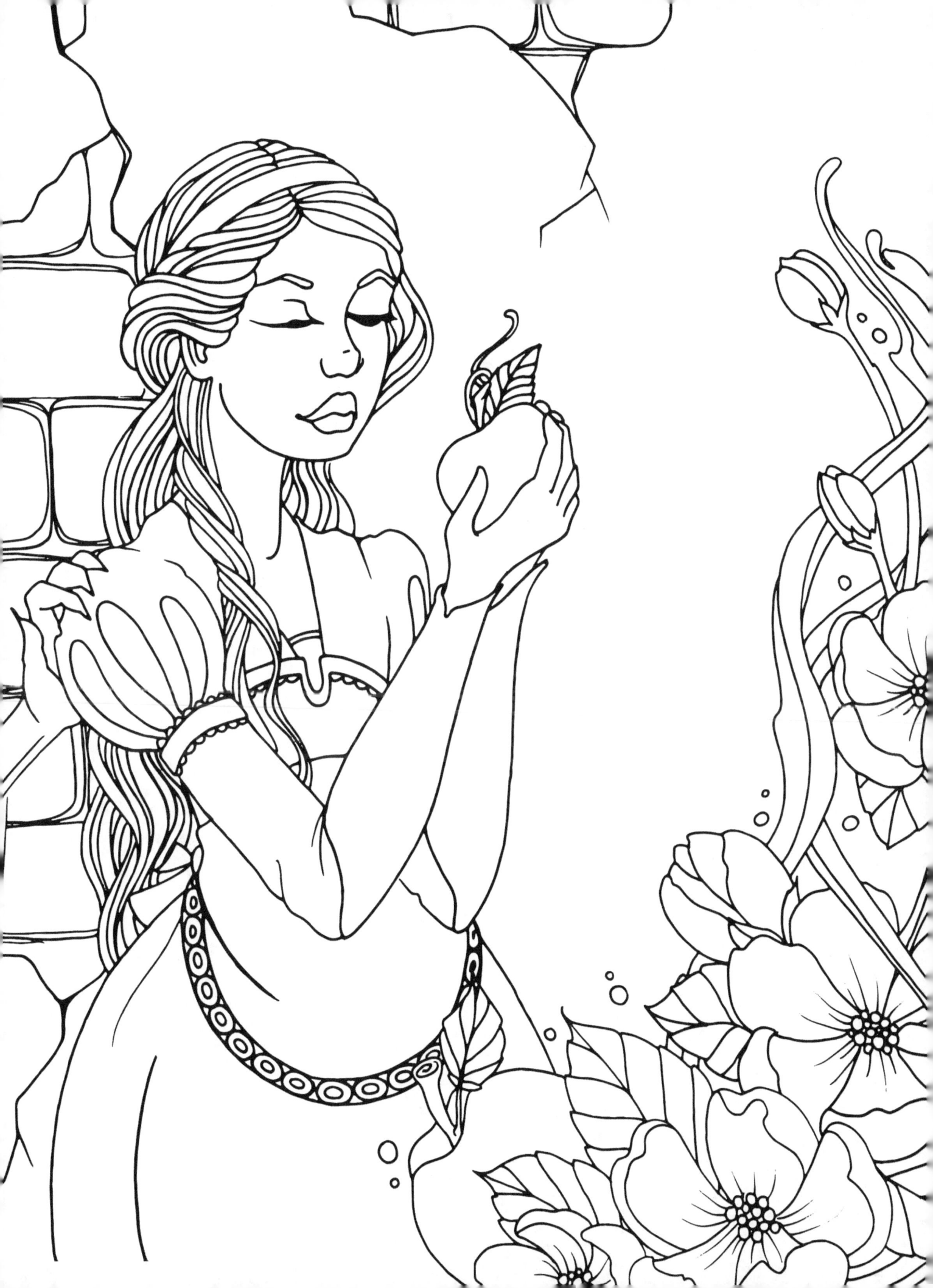

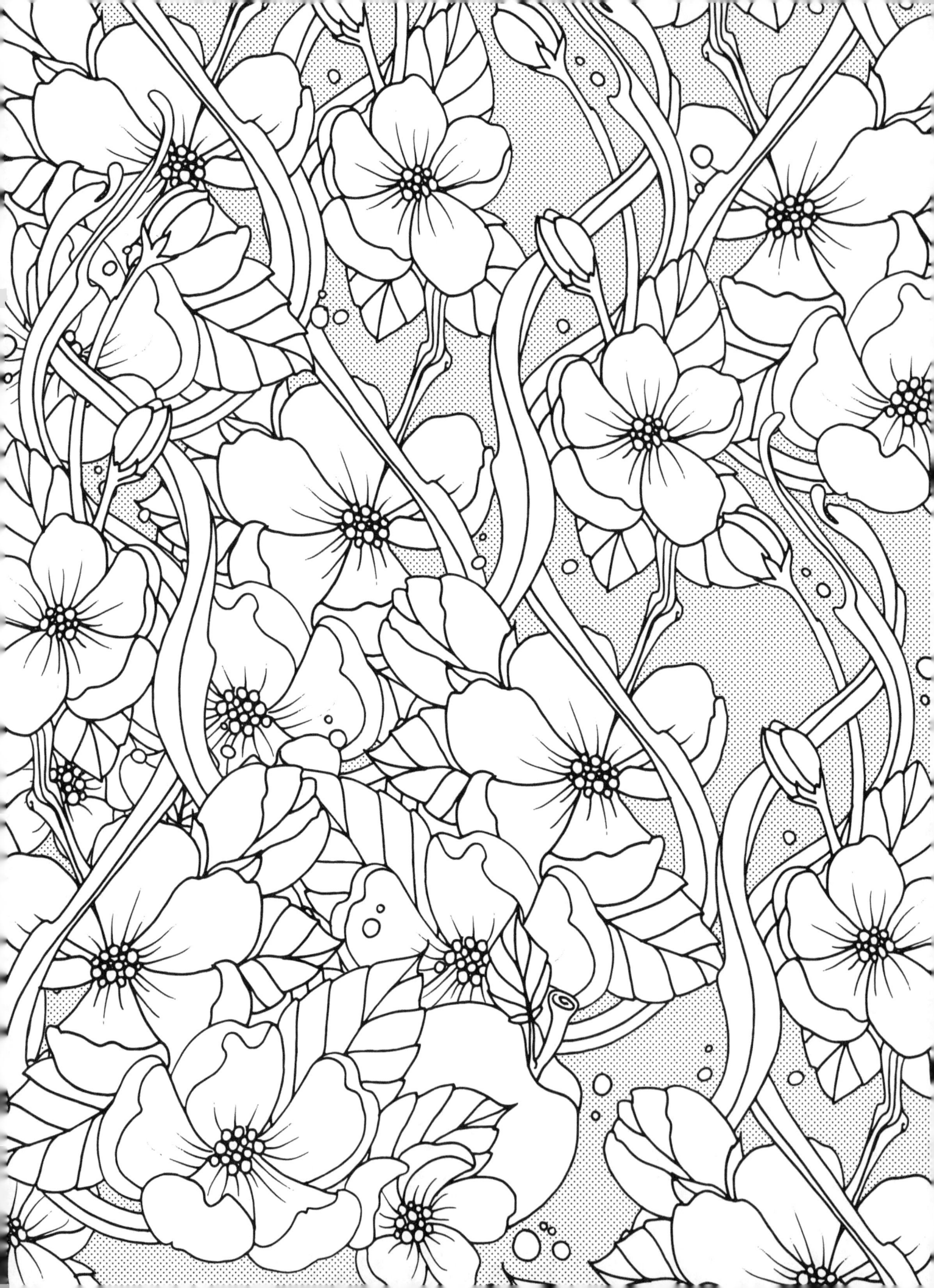

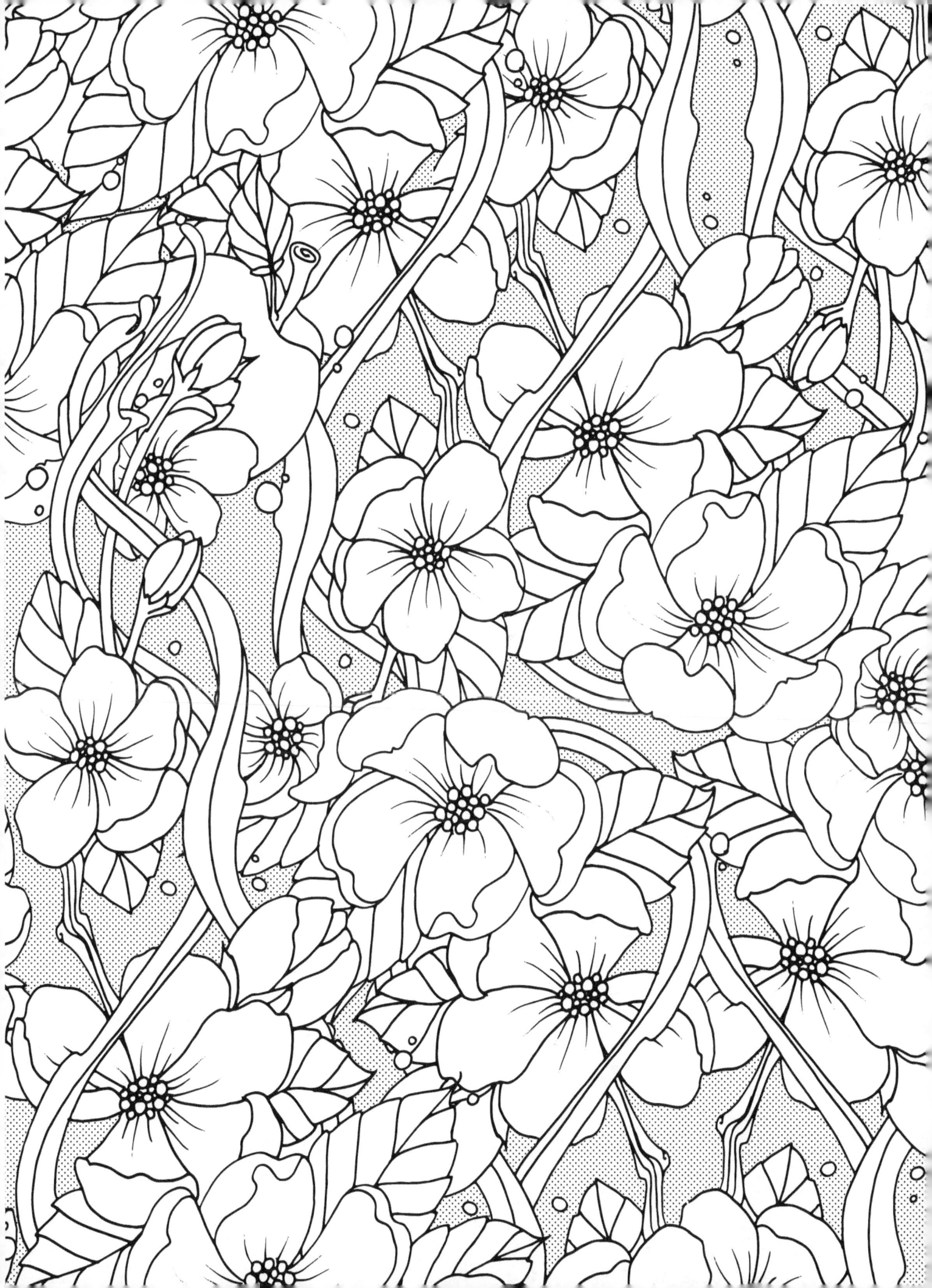

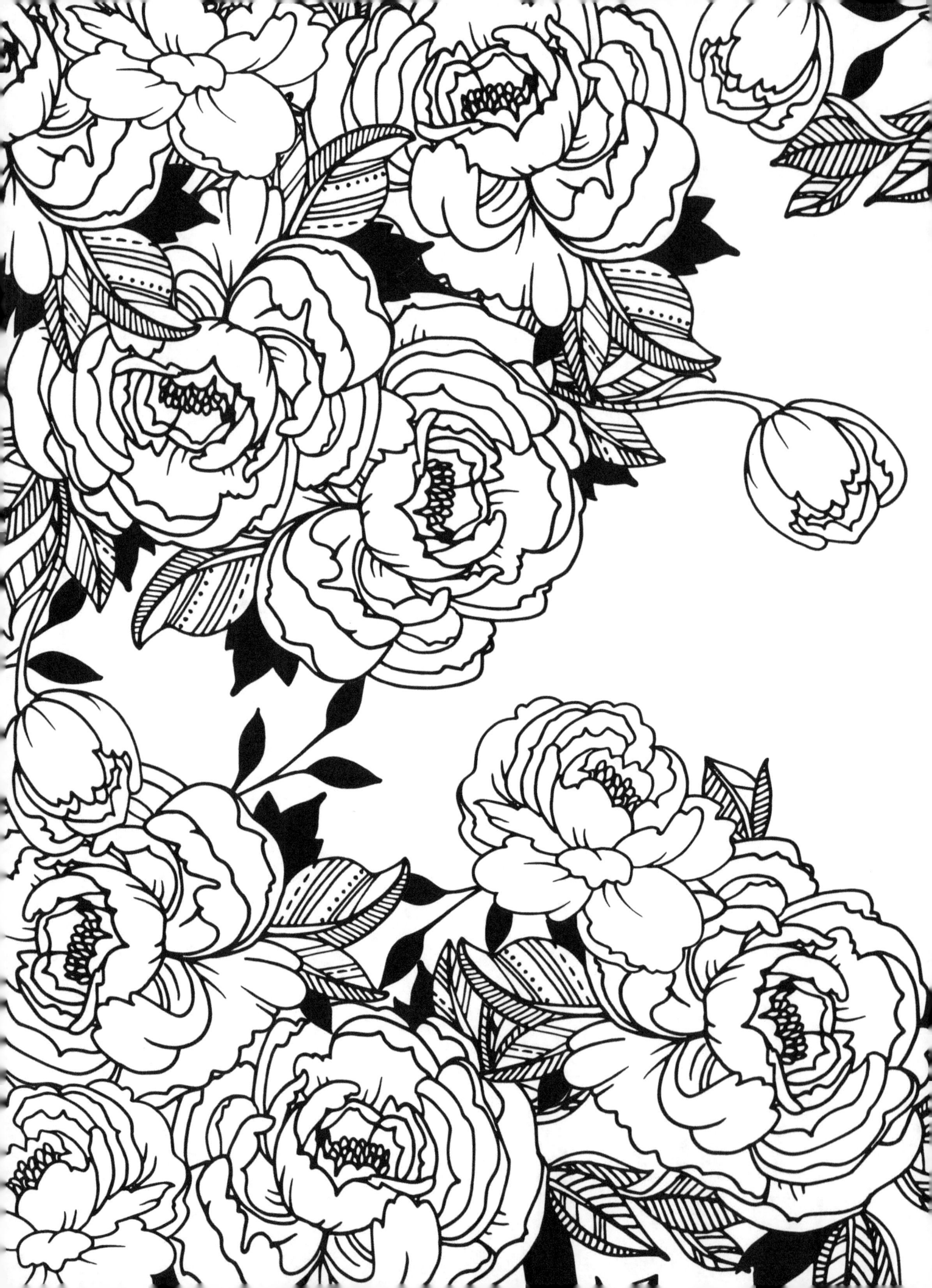

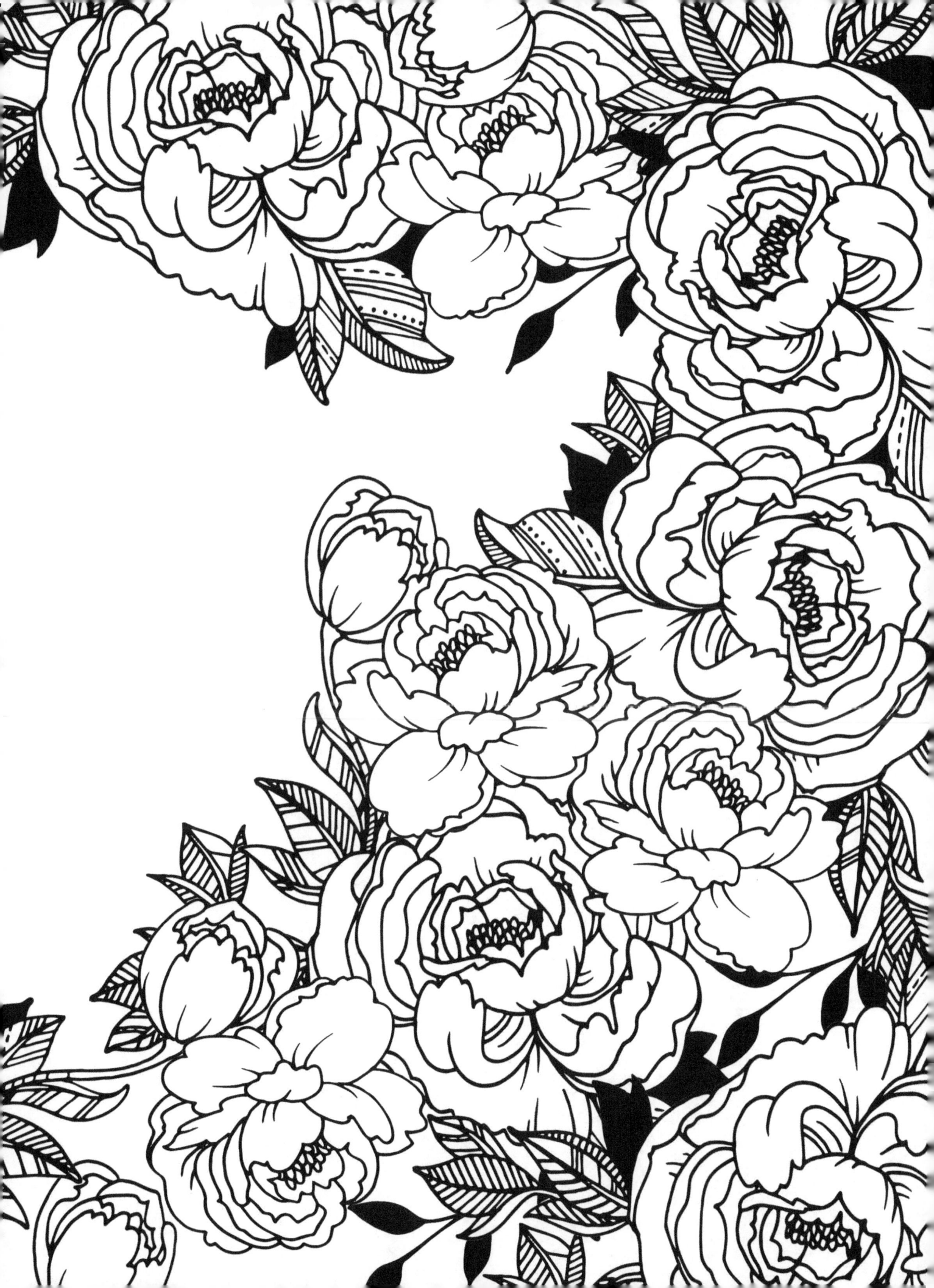

Sleeping Beauty

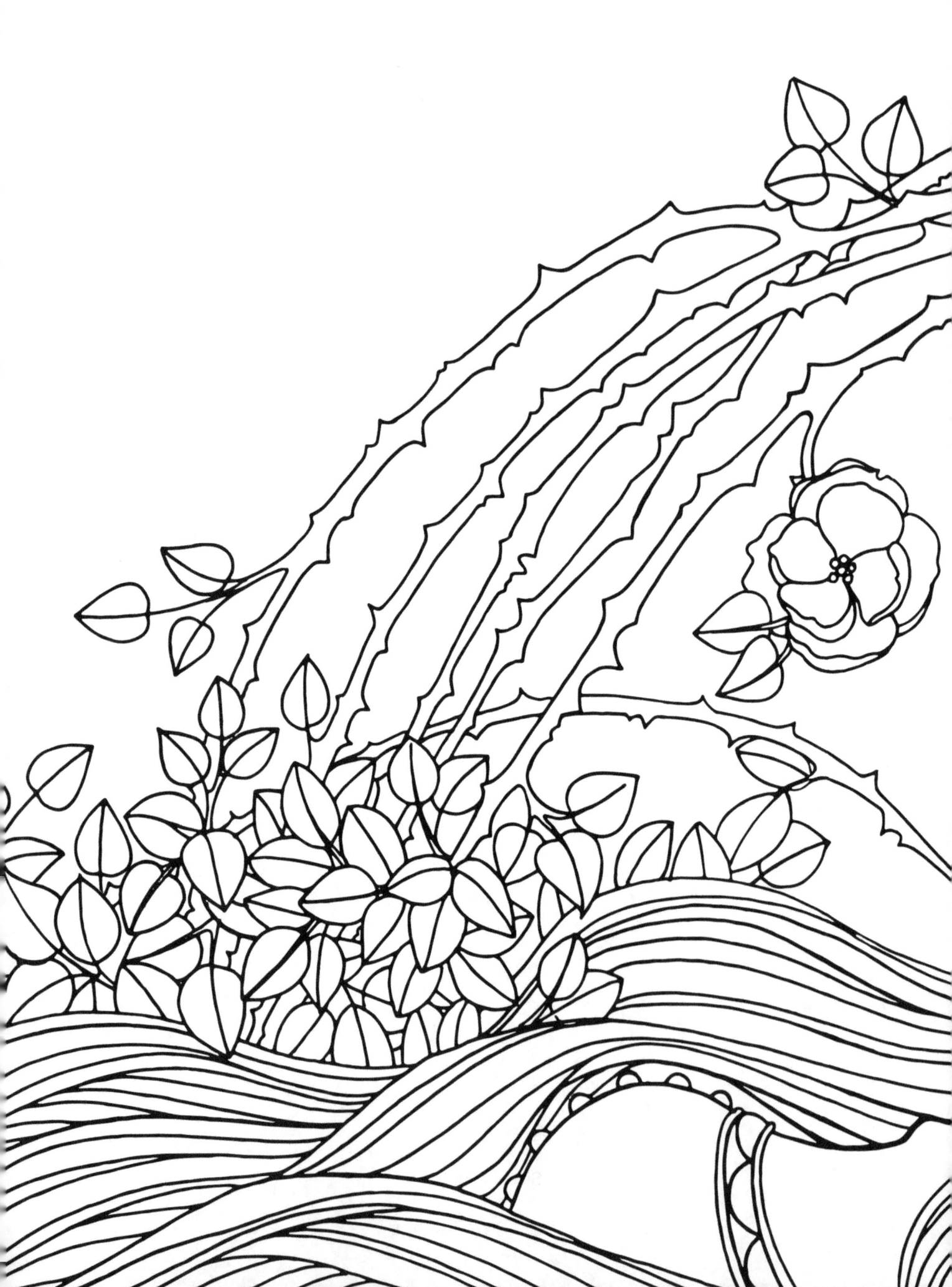

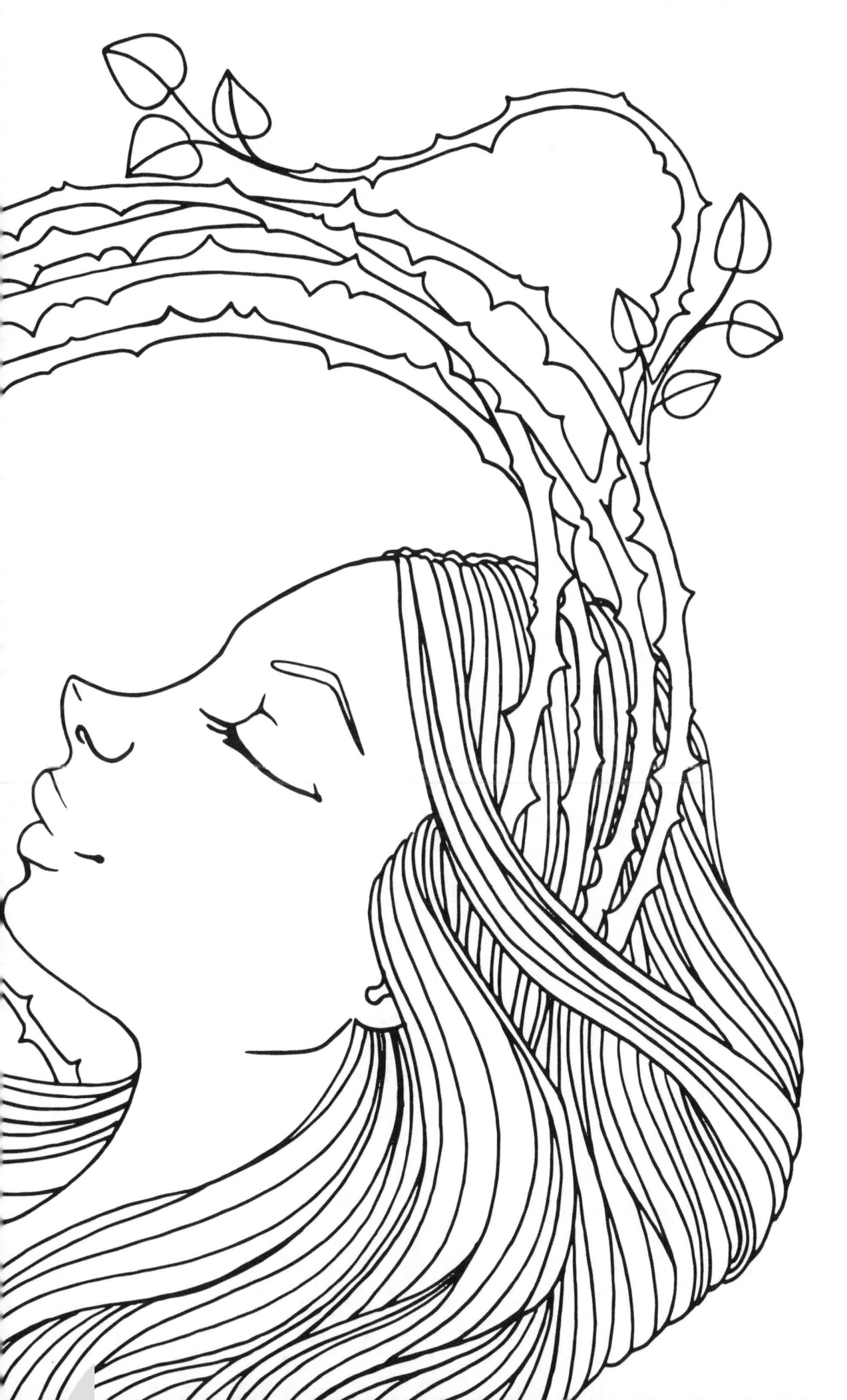

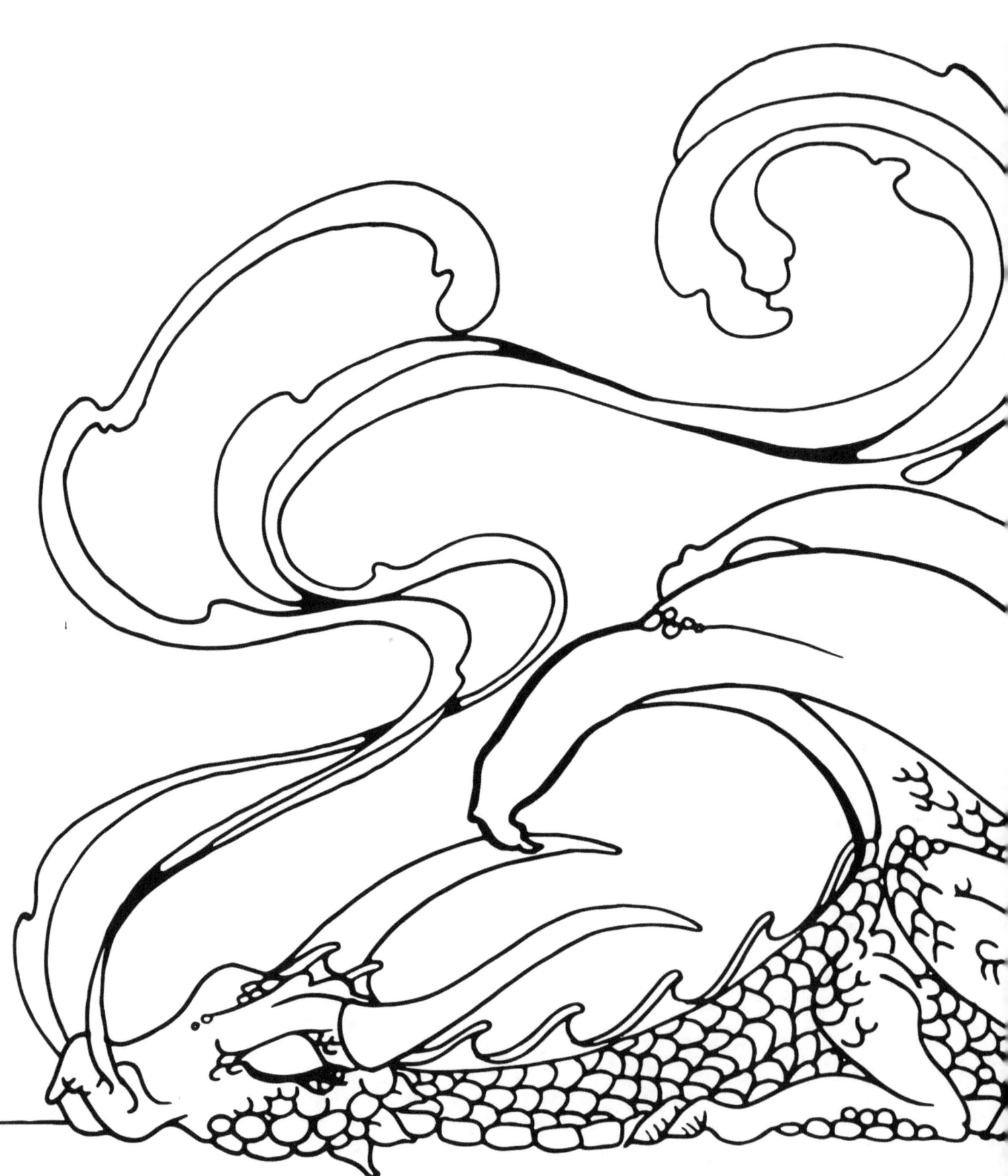

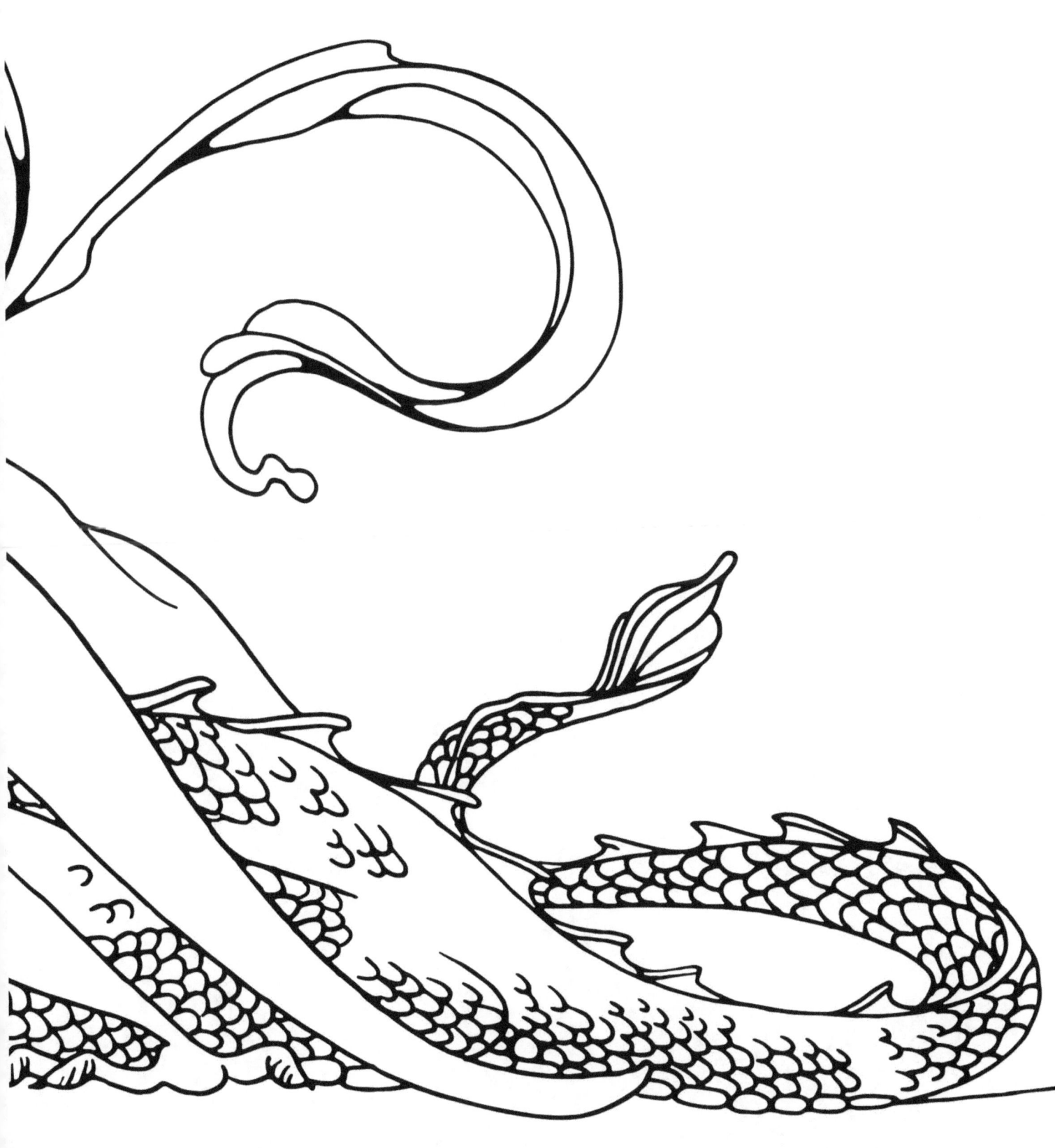

Princess and The Pea

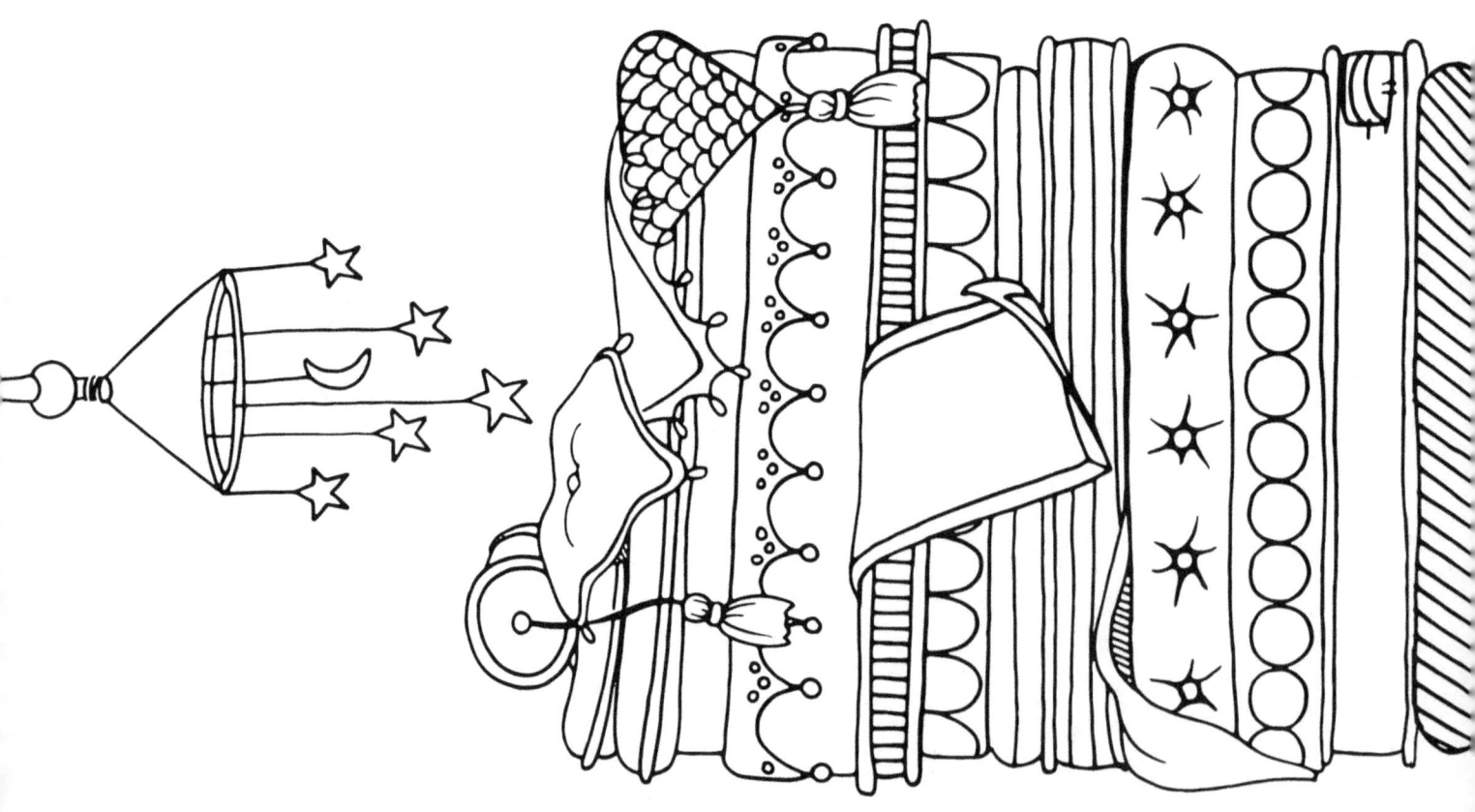

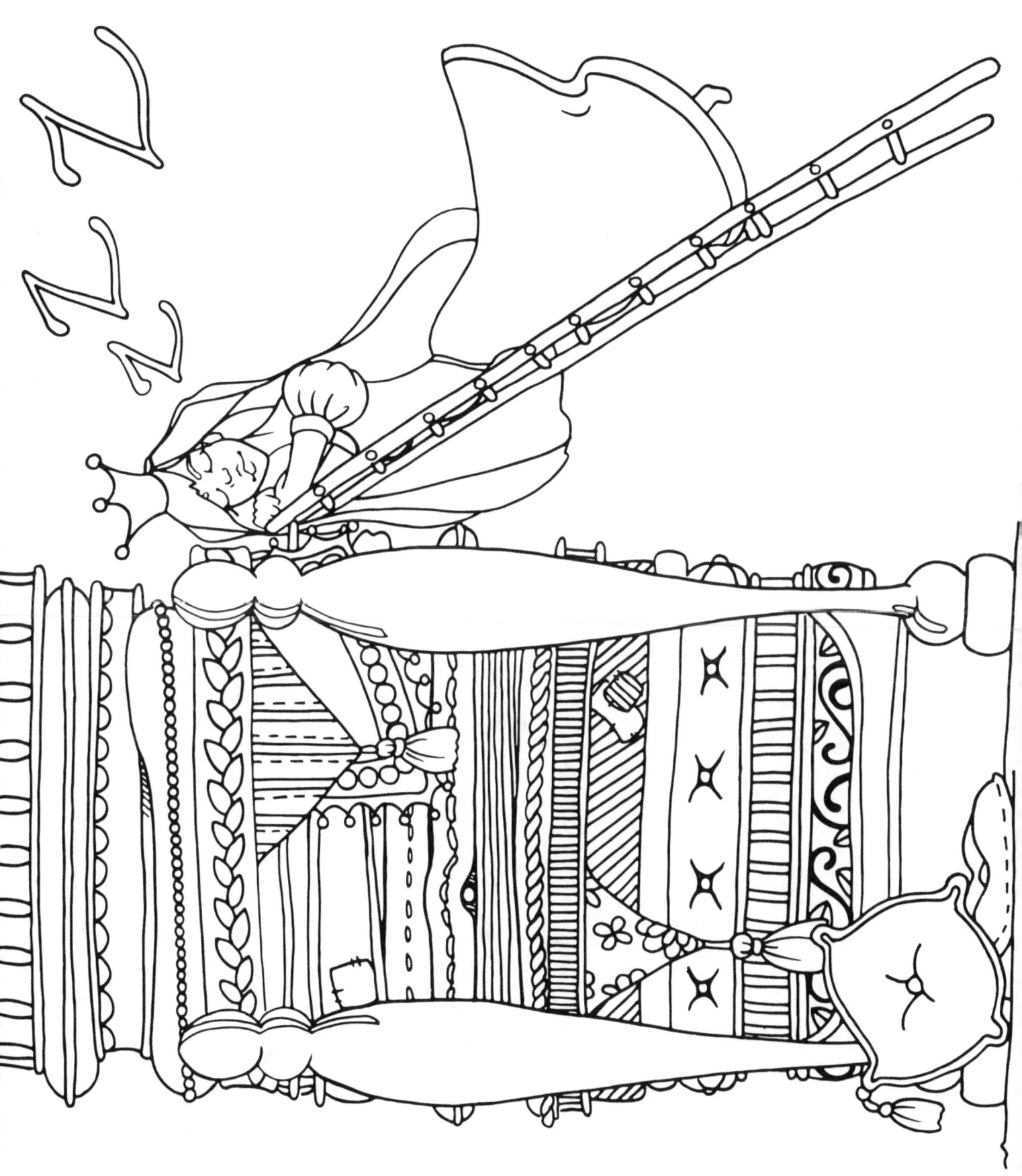

Goldie and Her three Bears
Create your own texture and fur.

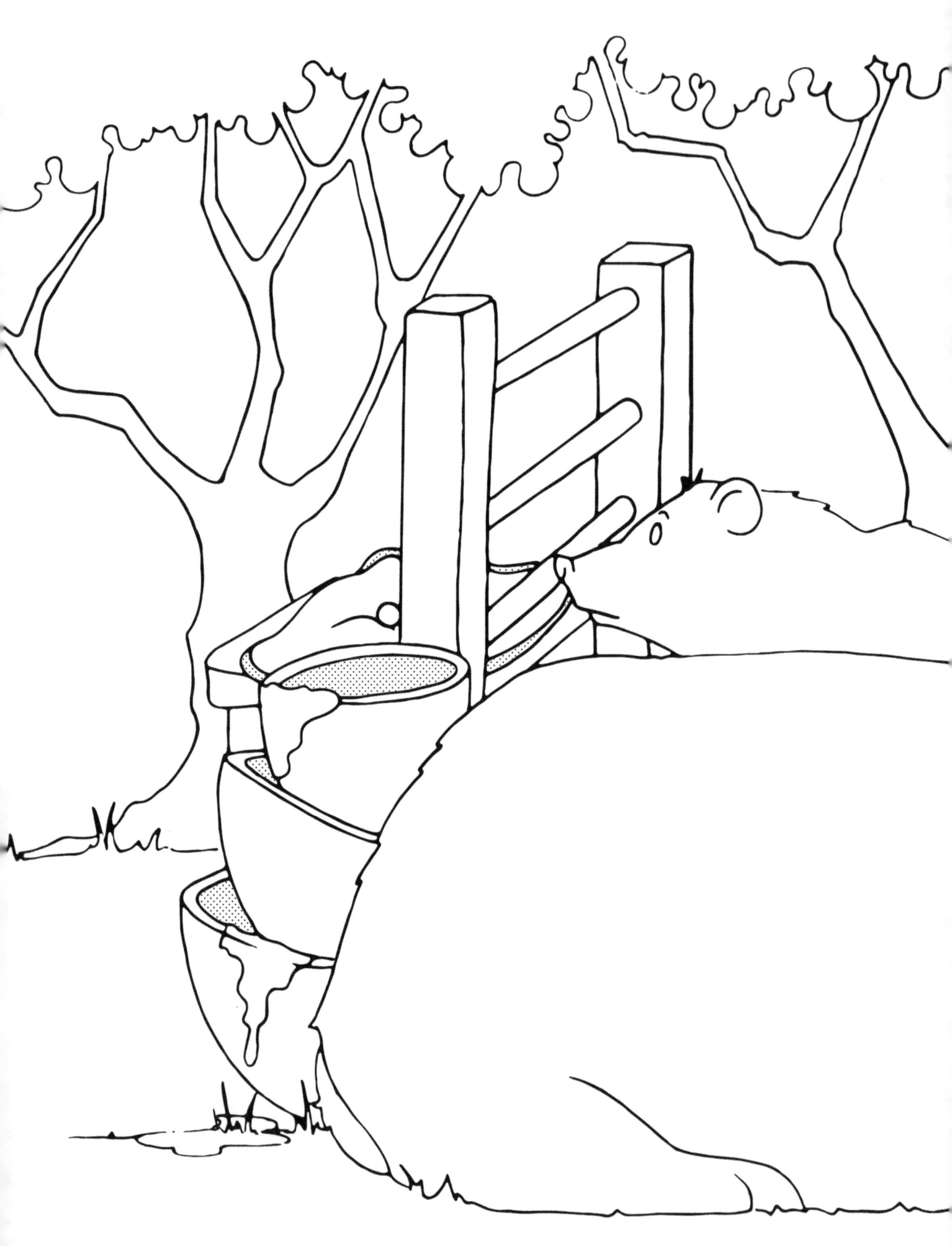

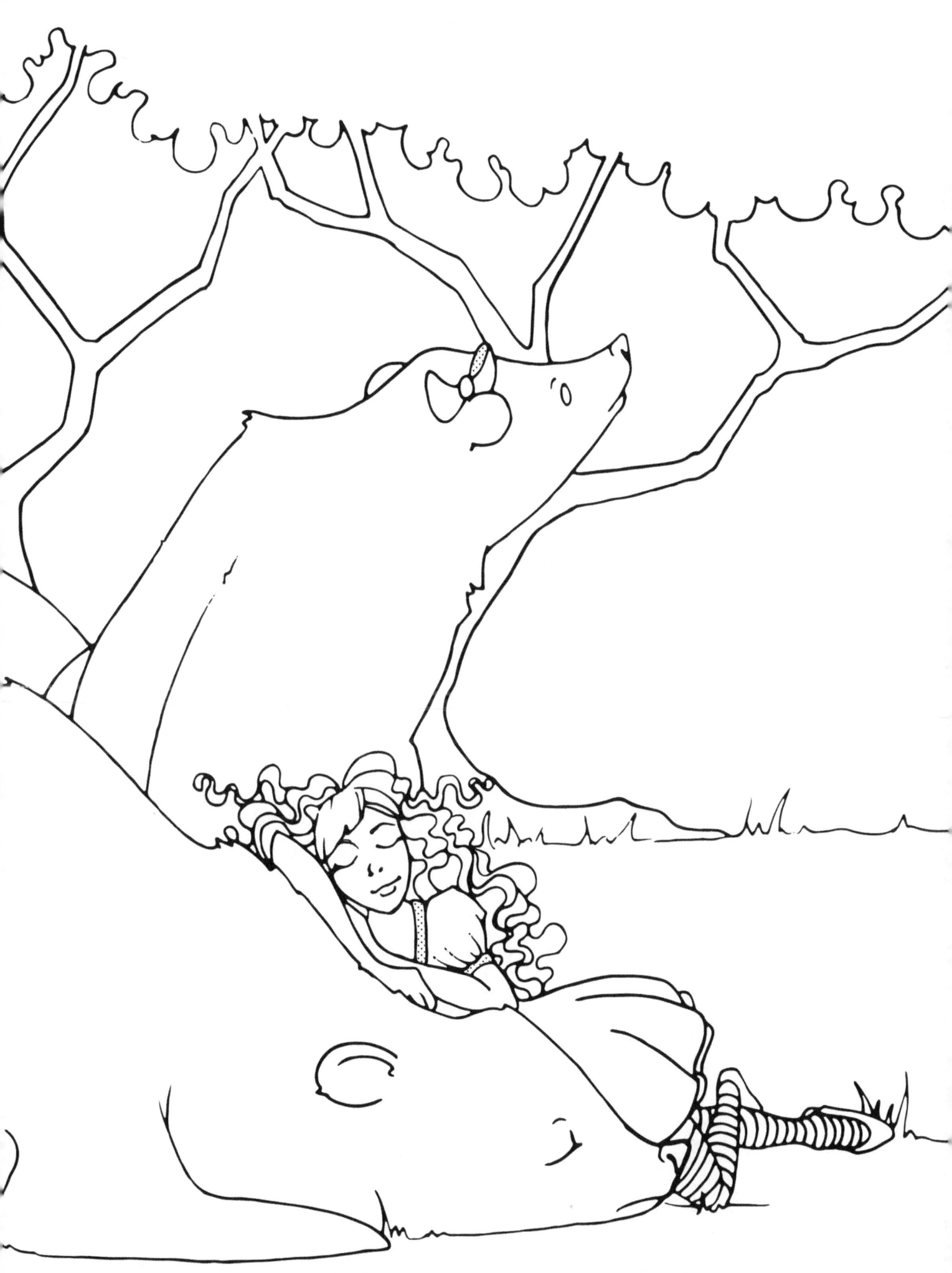

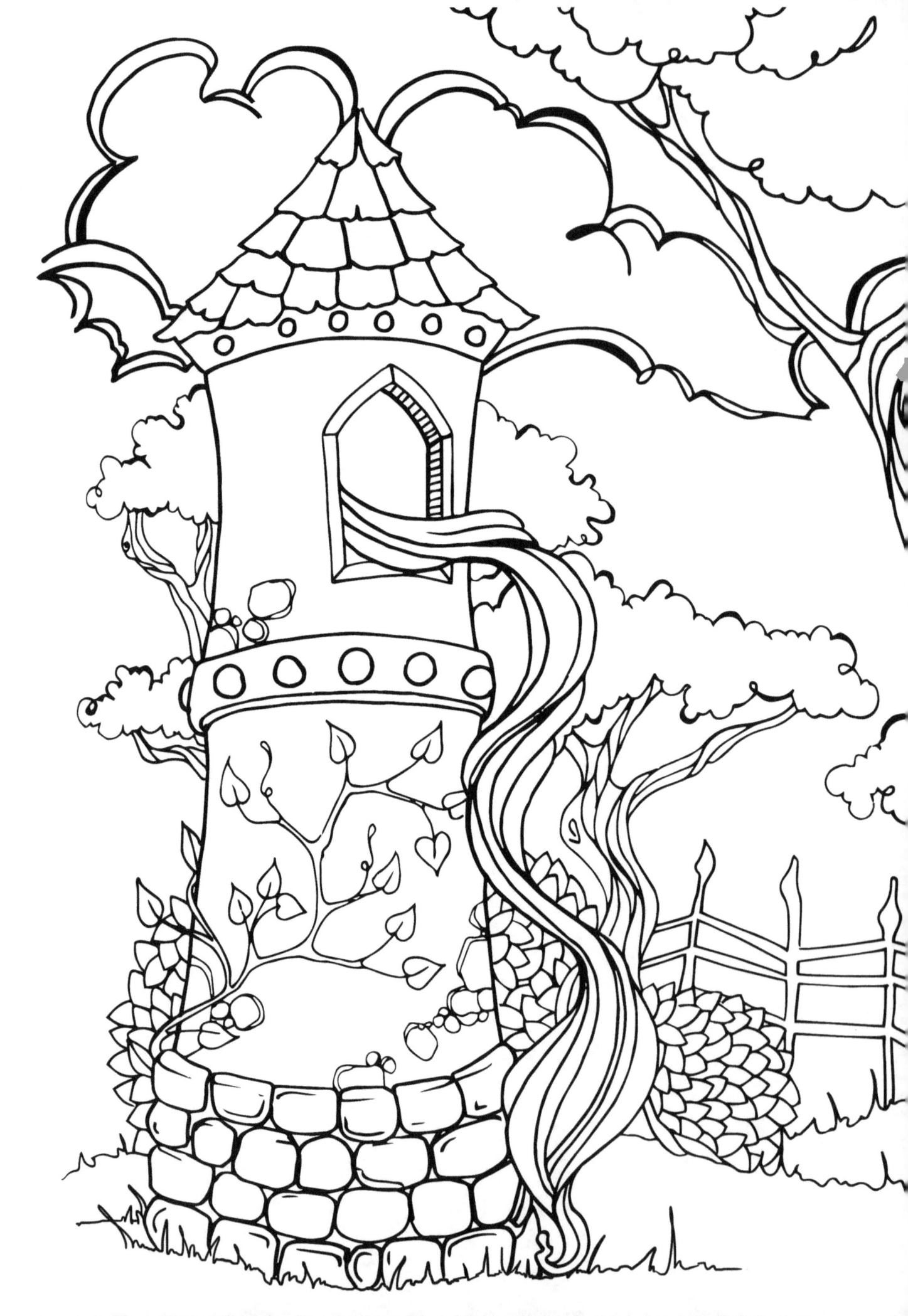

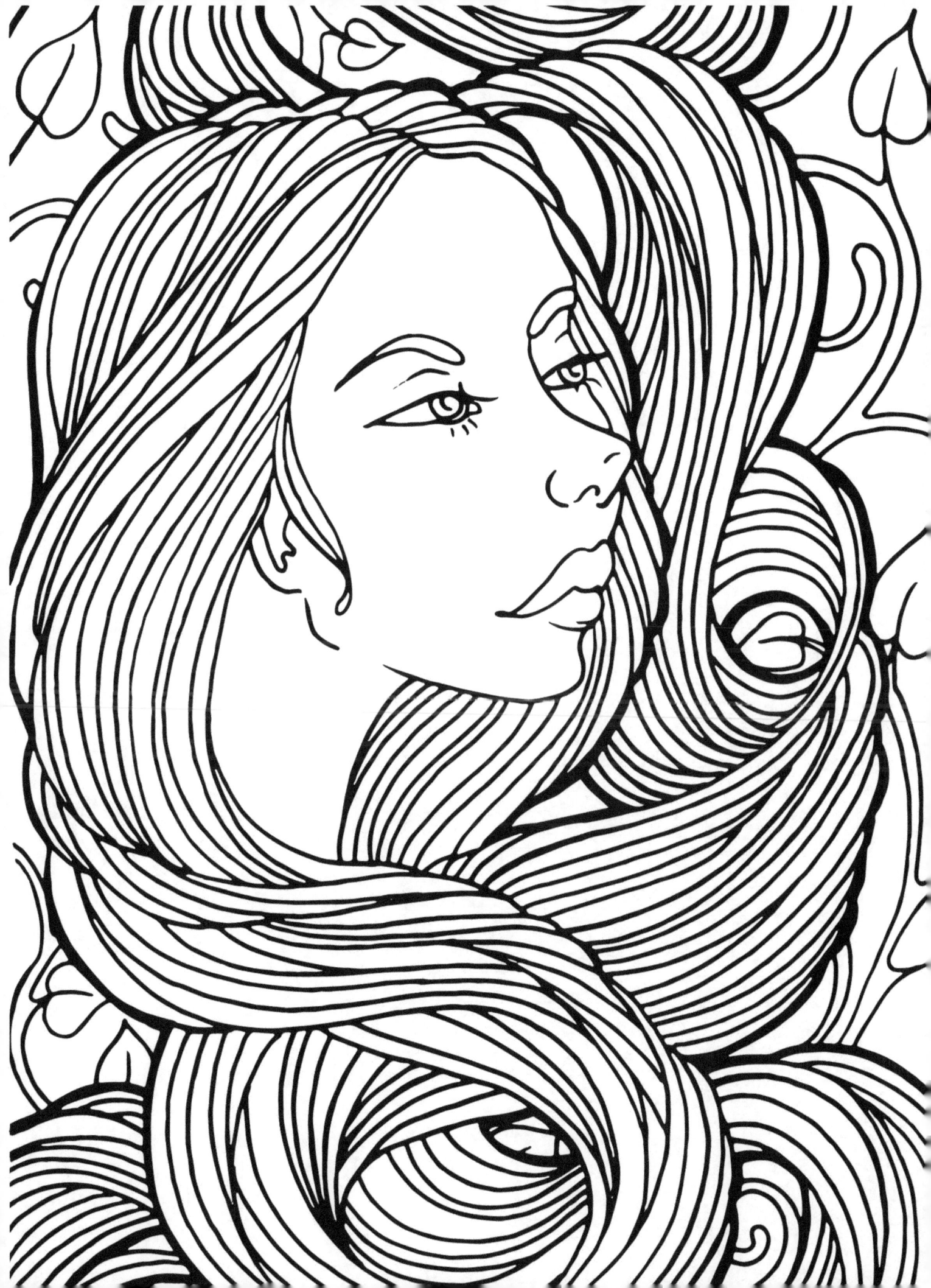

Little Mermaid

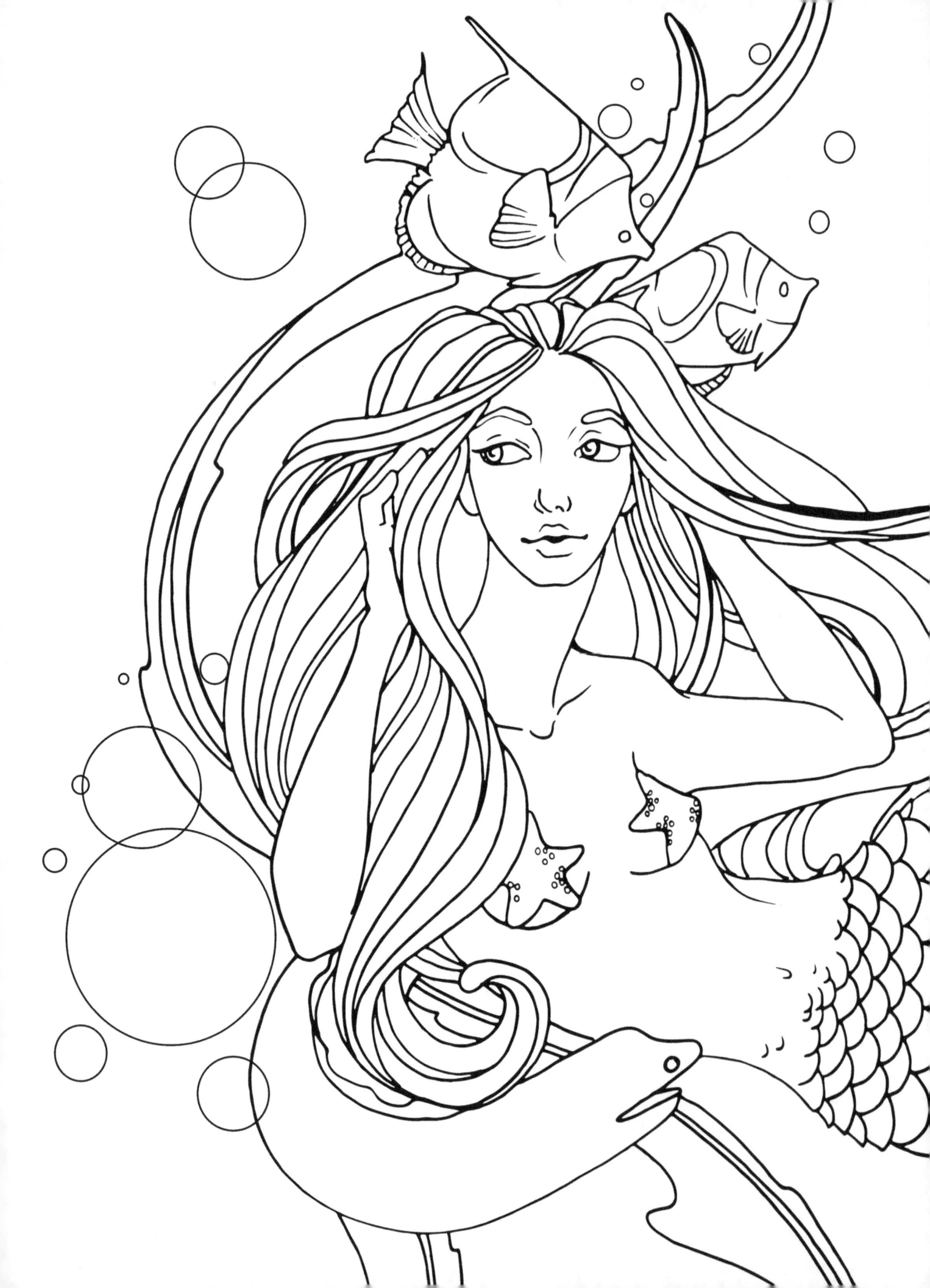

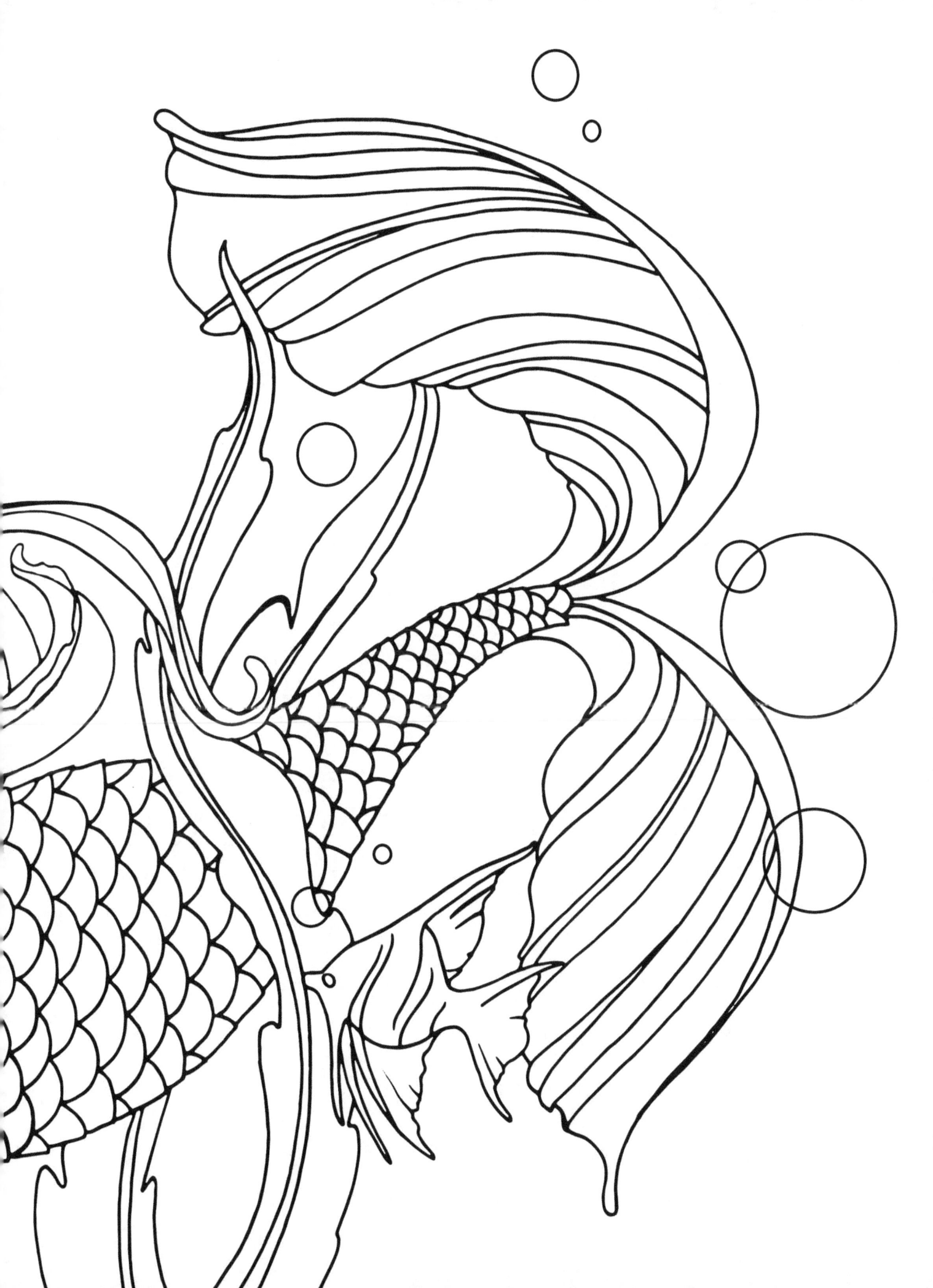

Cinderella

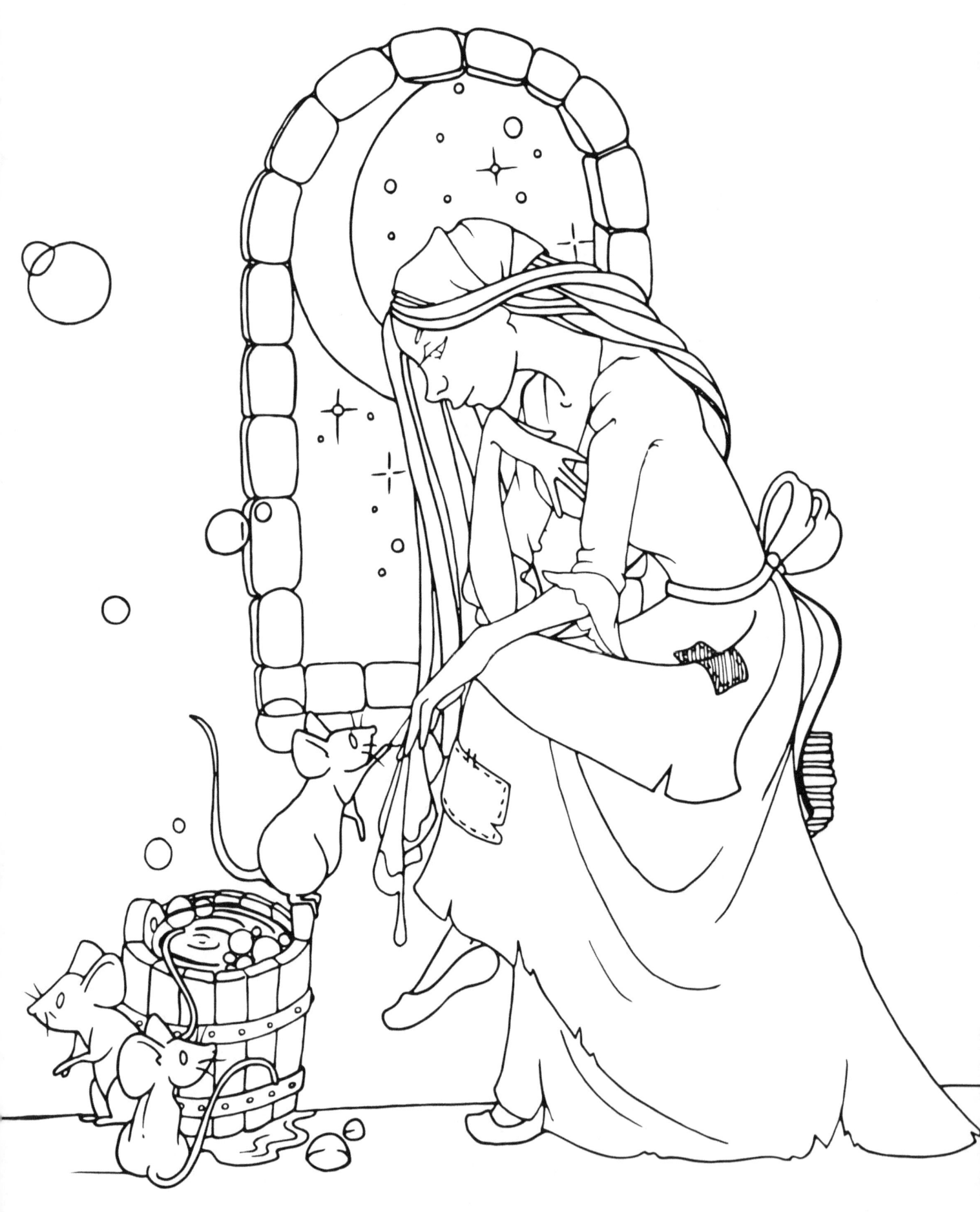

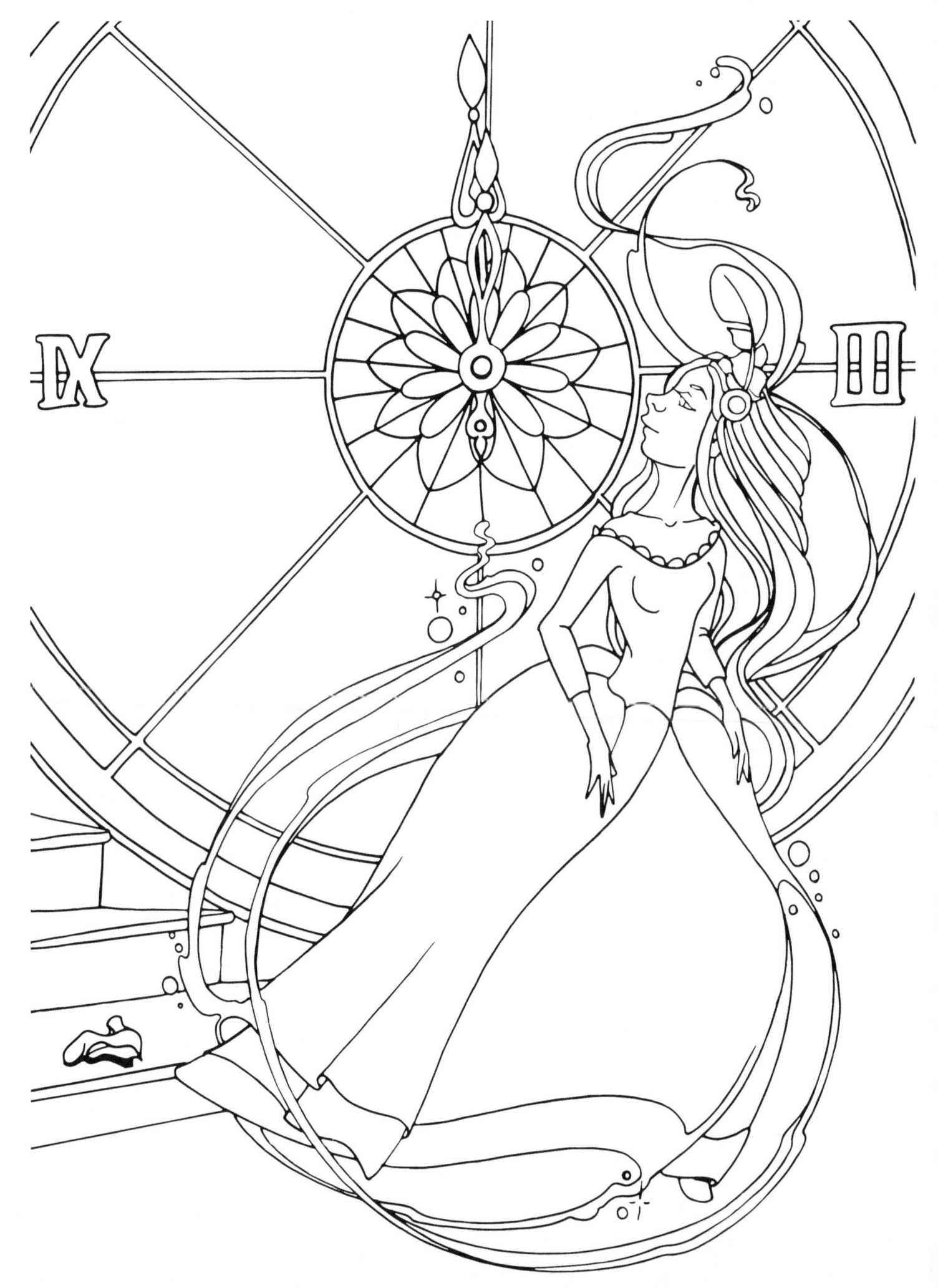

Blue Beard

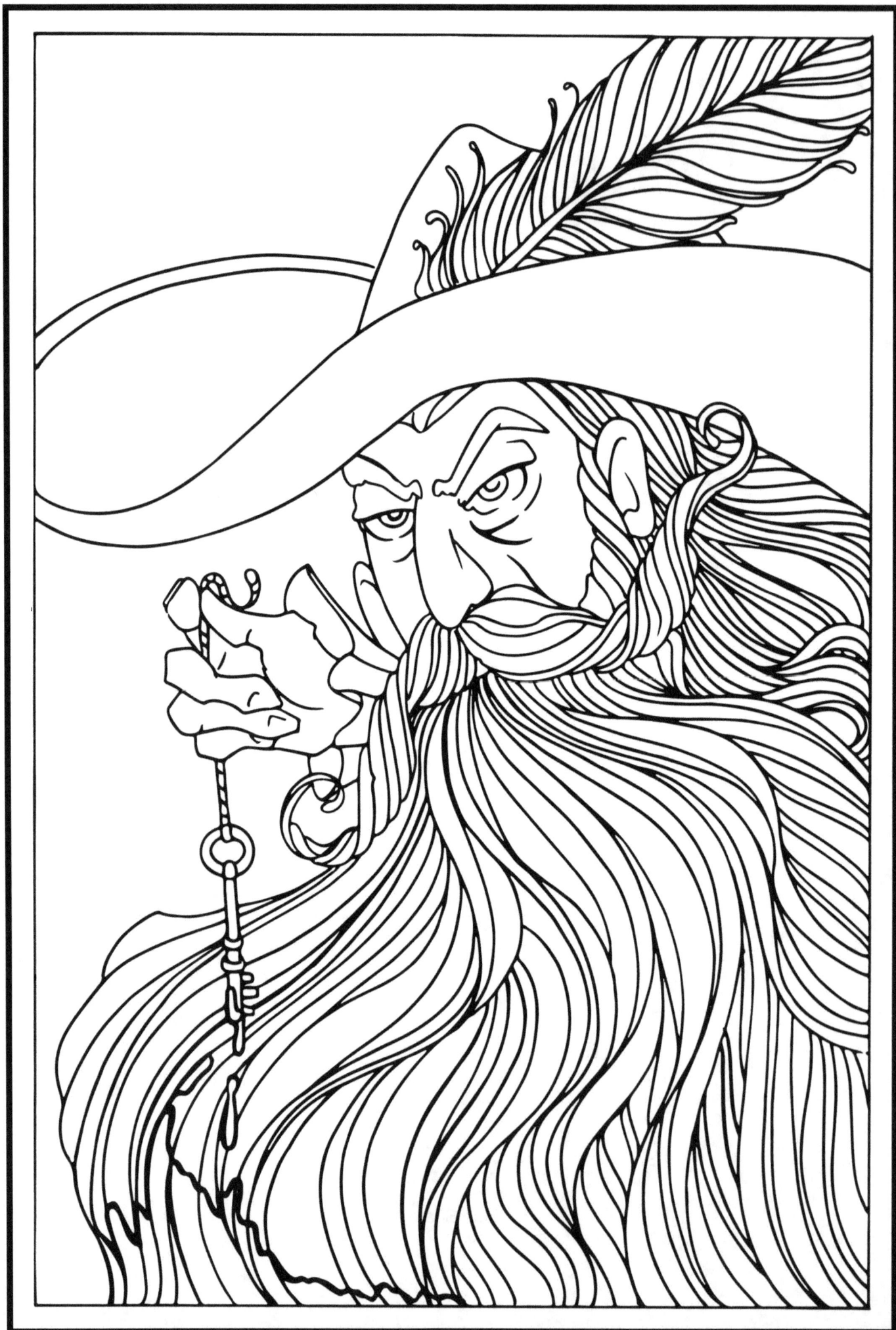

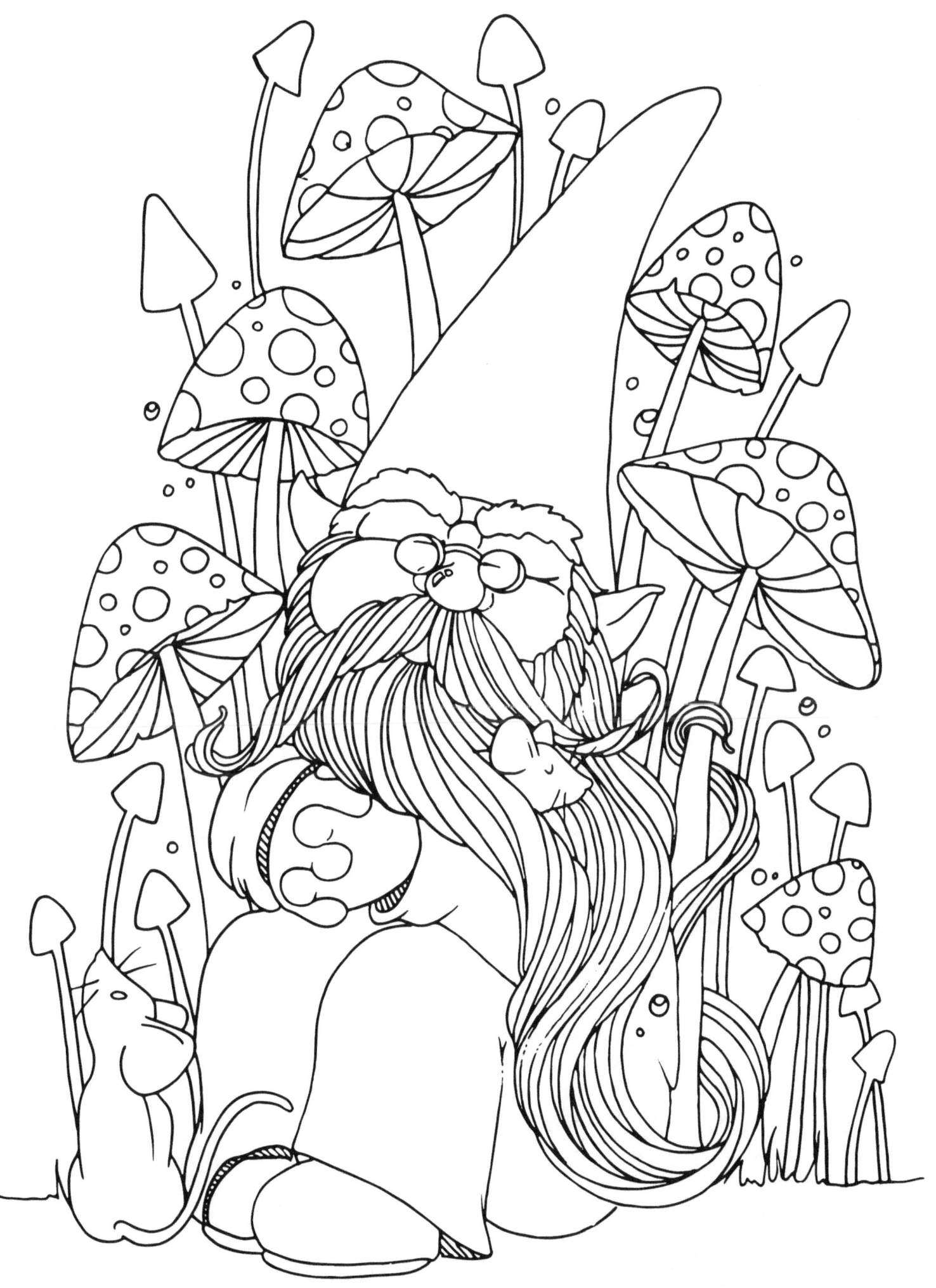

Gnome More Sleep

The Juniper Tree

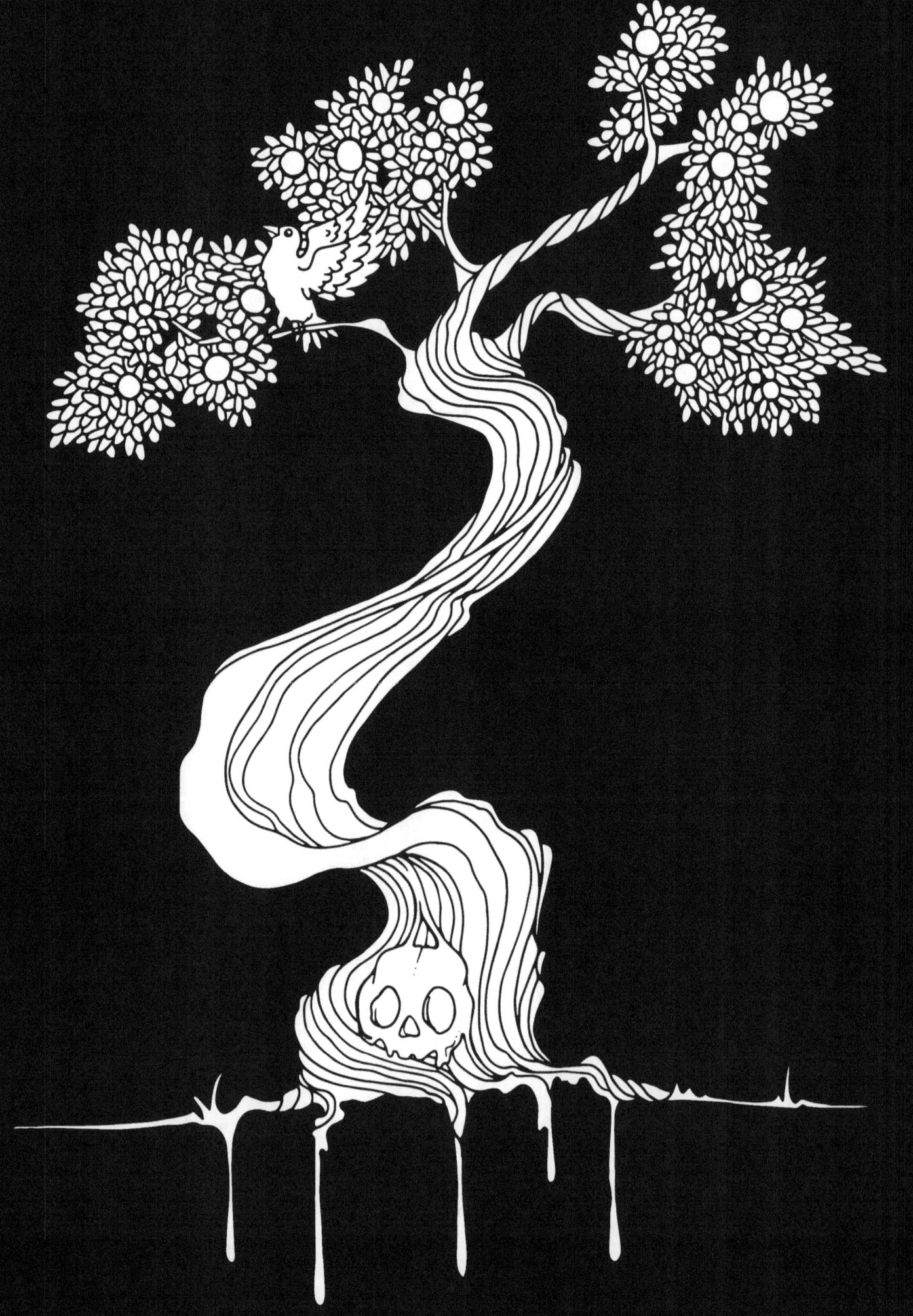

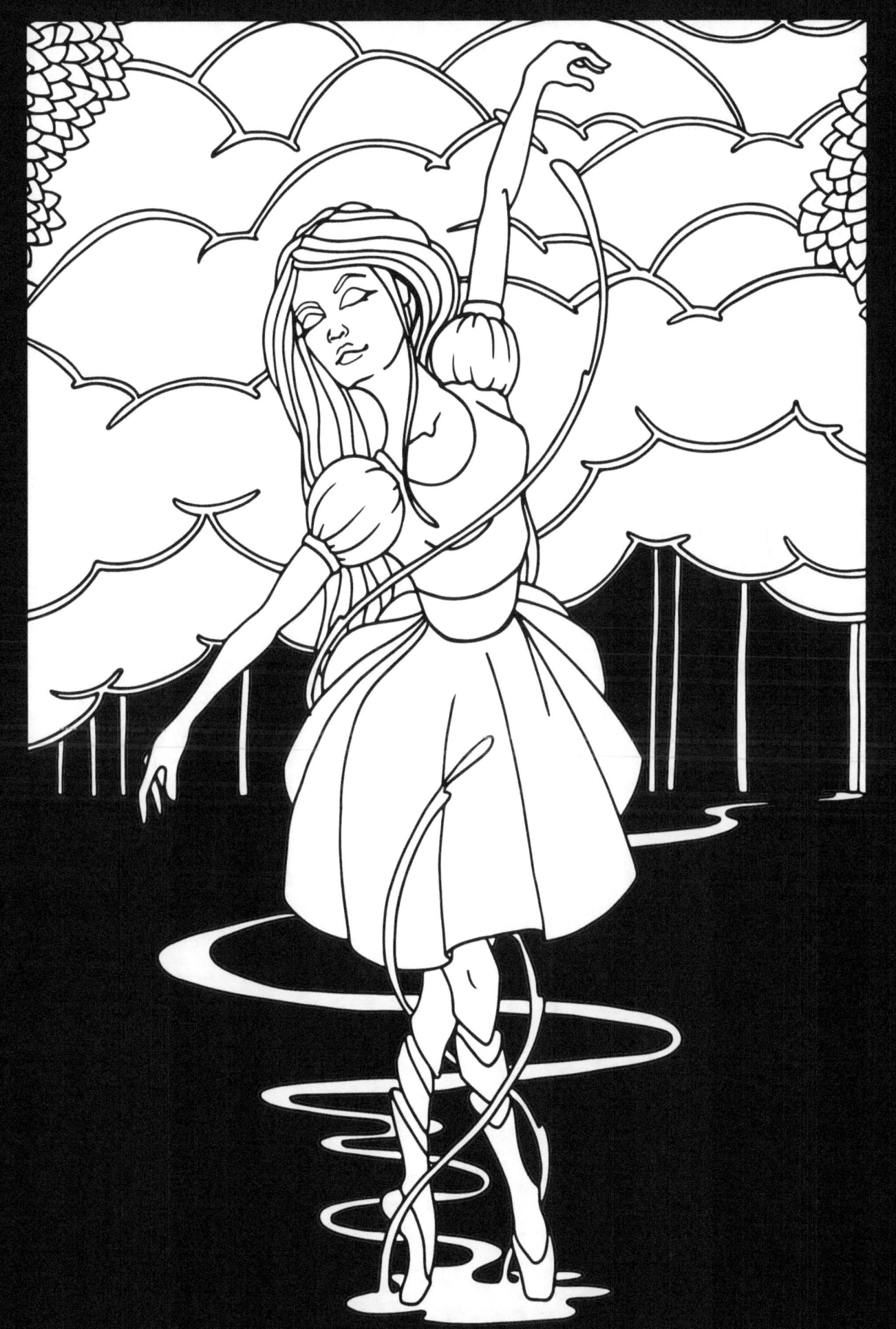

The Red Shoes

Spring Fairy

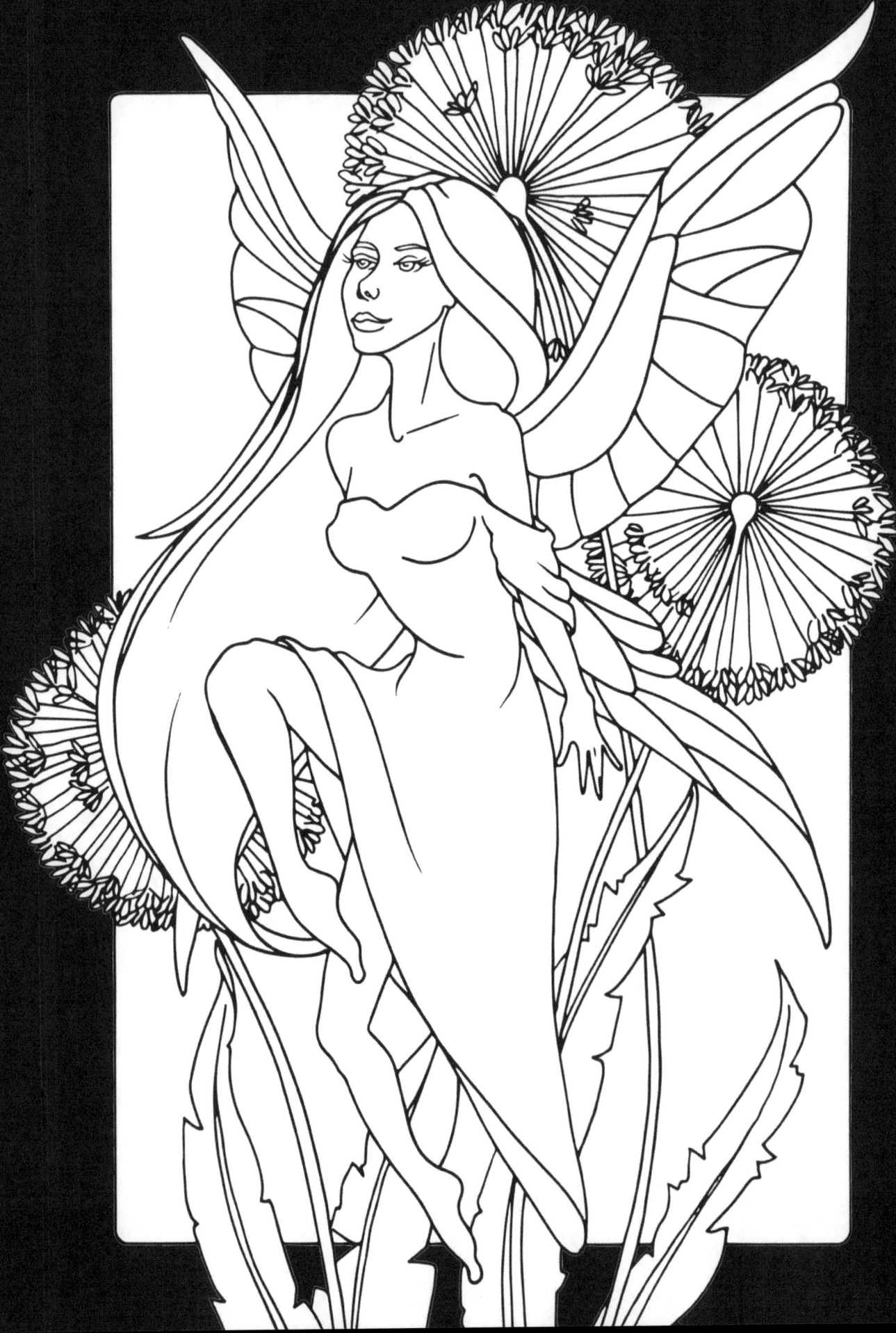

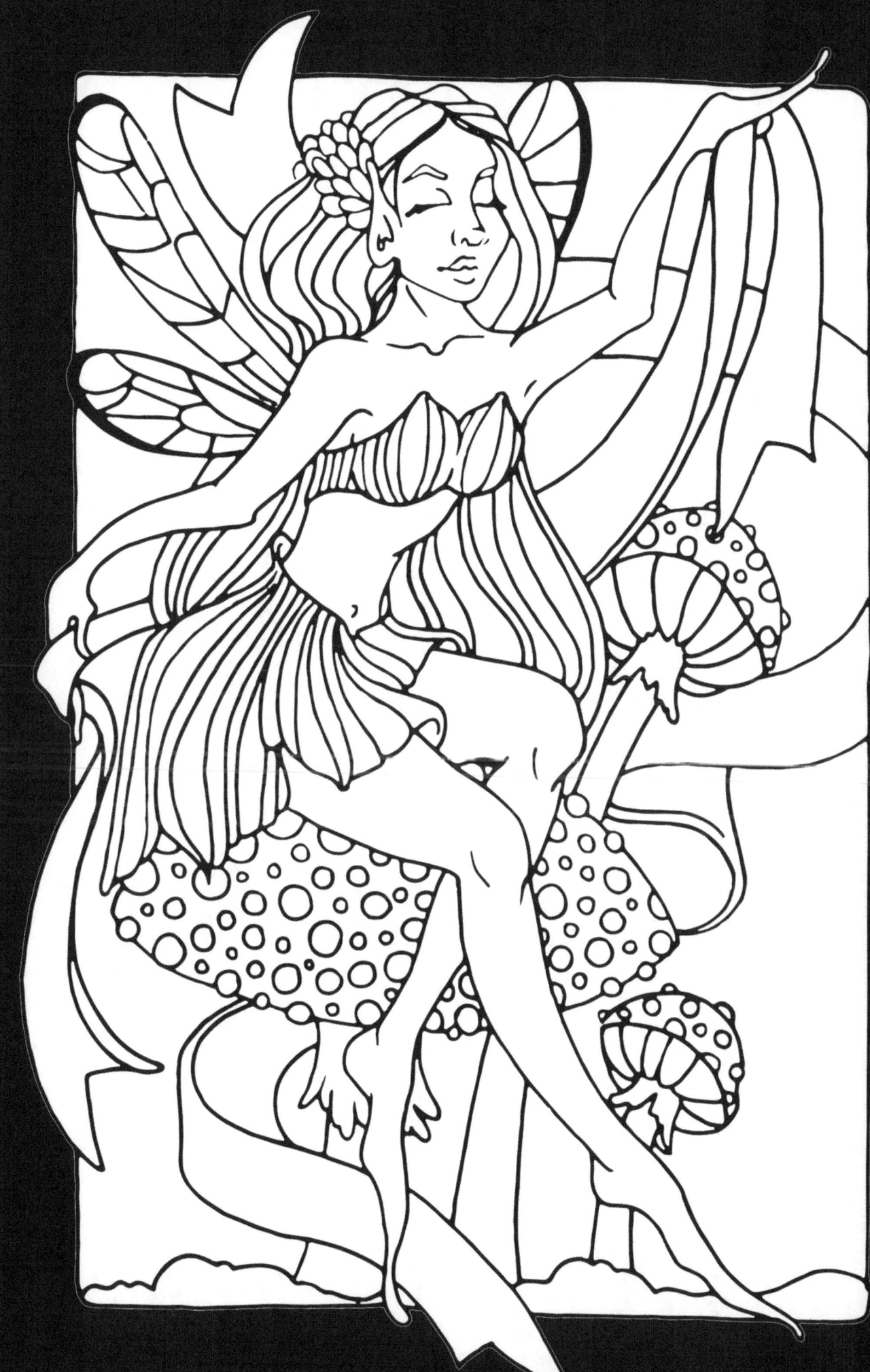

Woodland Fairy

Peyton

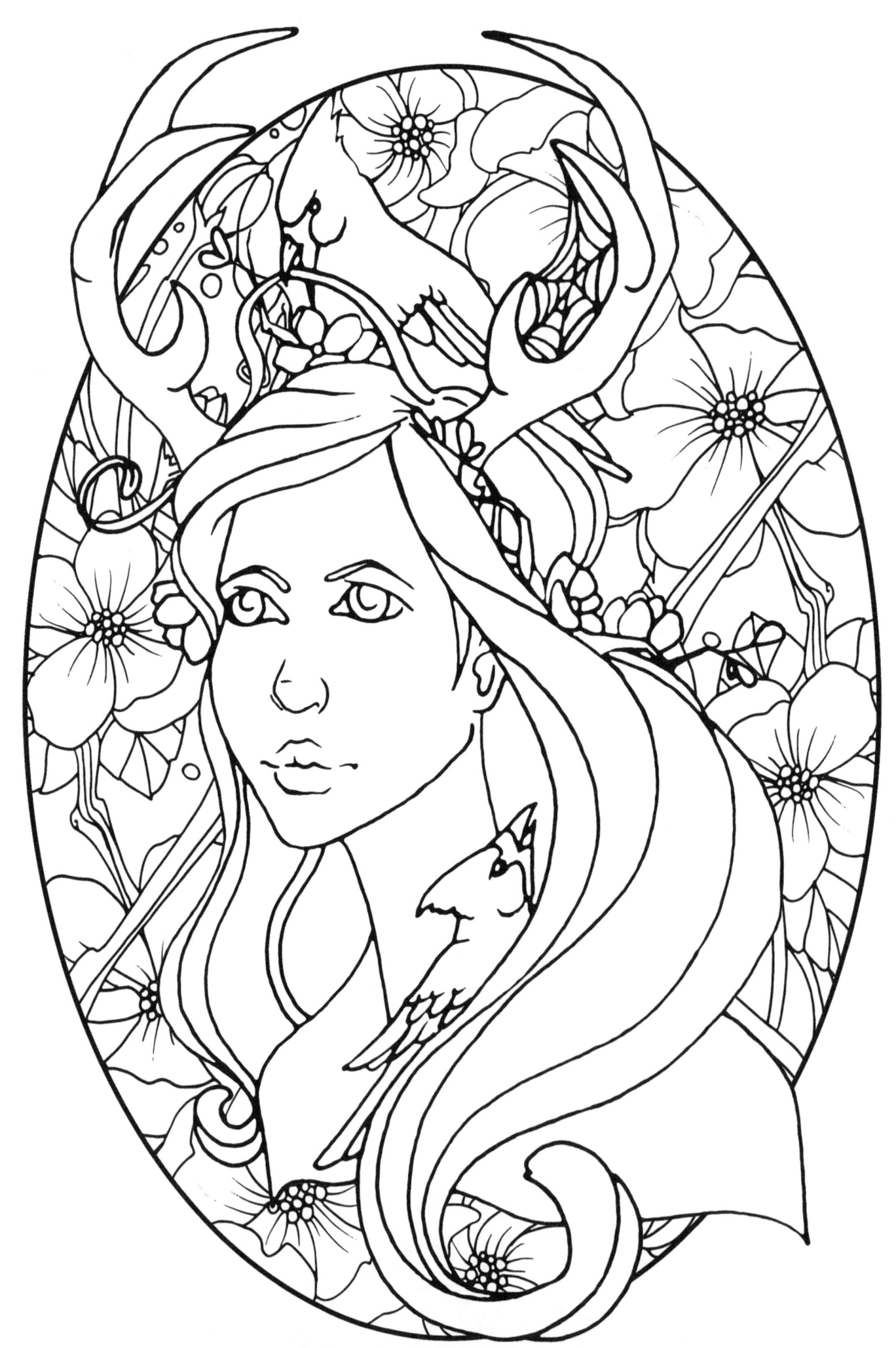

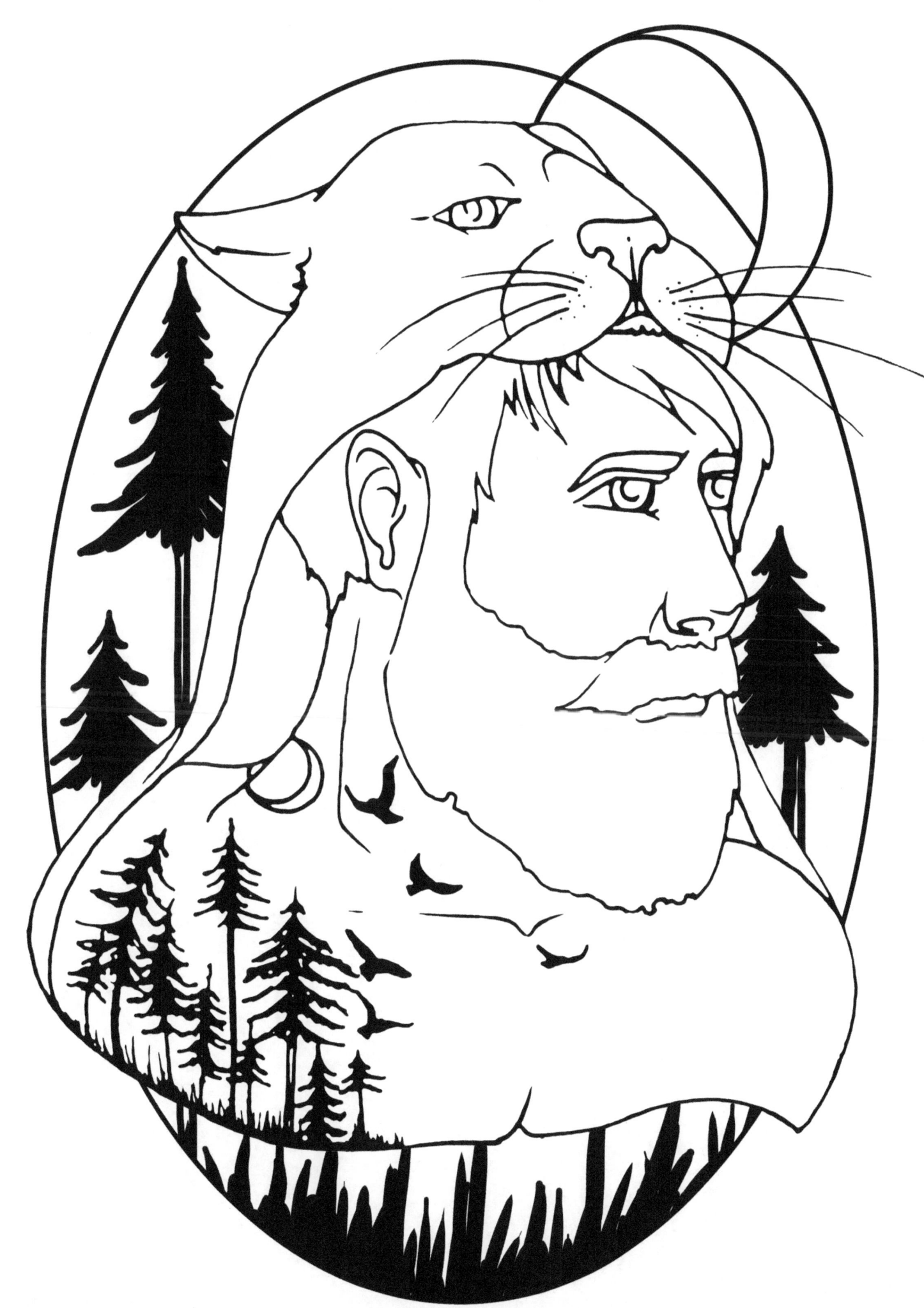

Sphen

Ugly Duckling

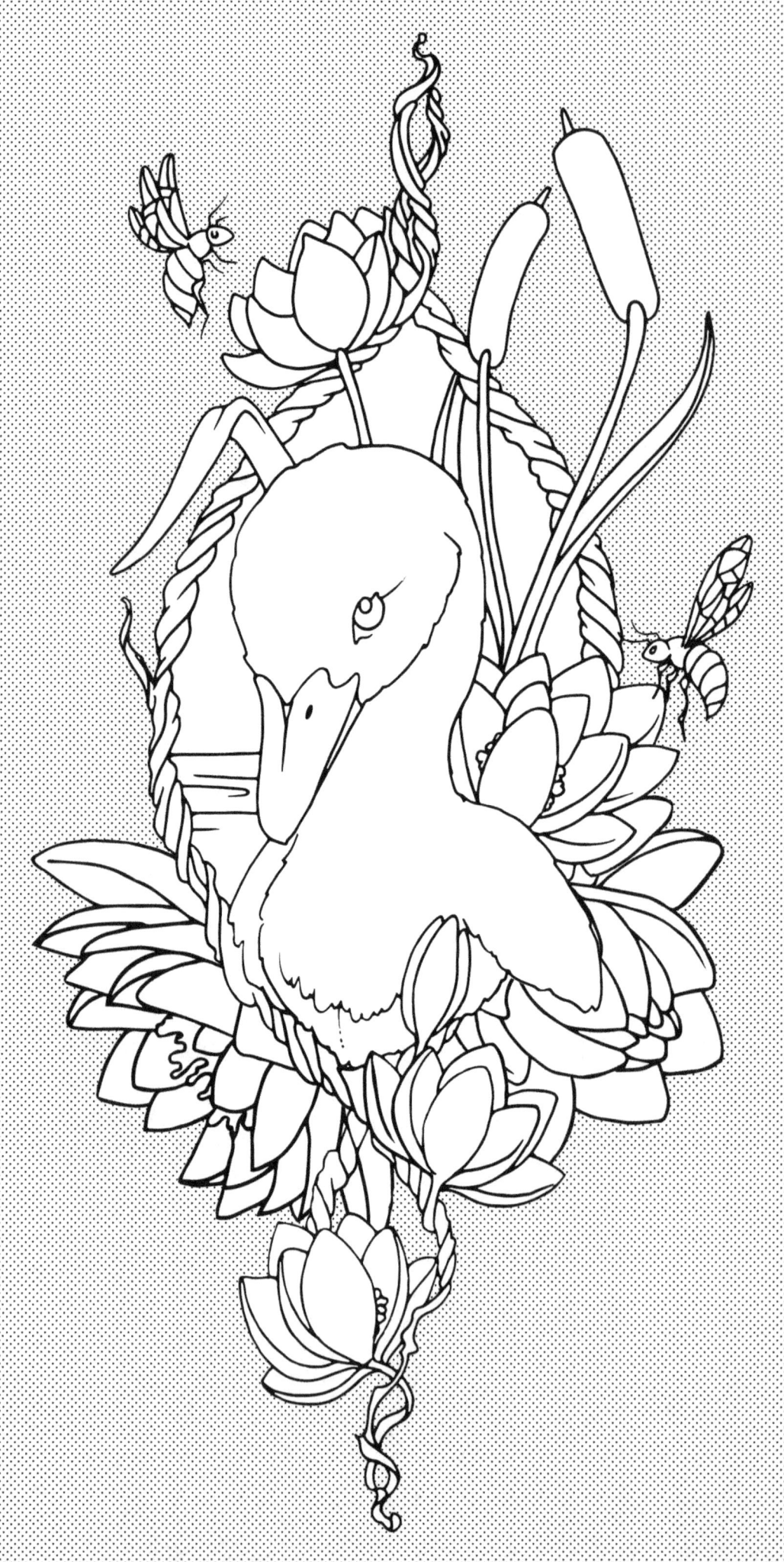

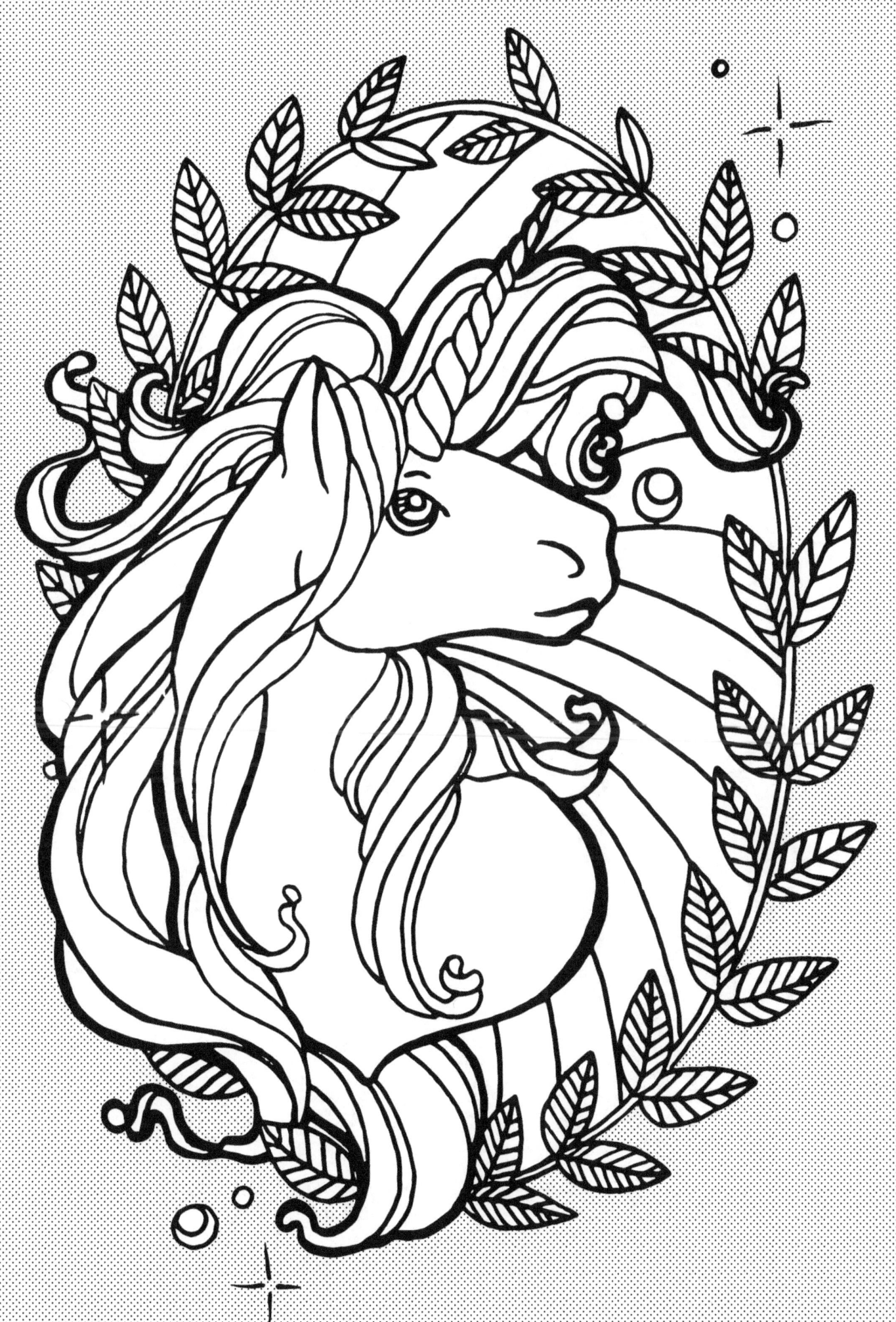

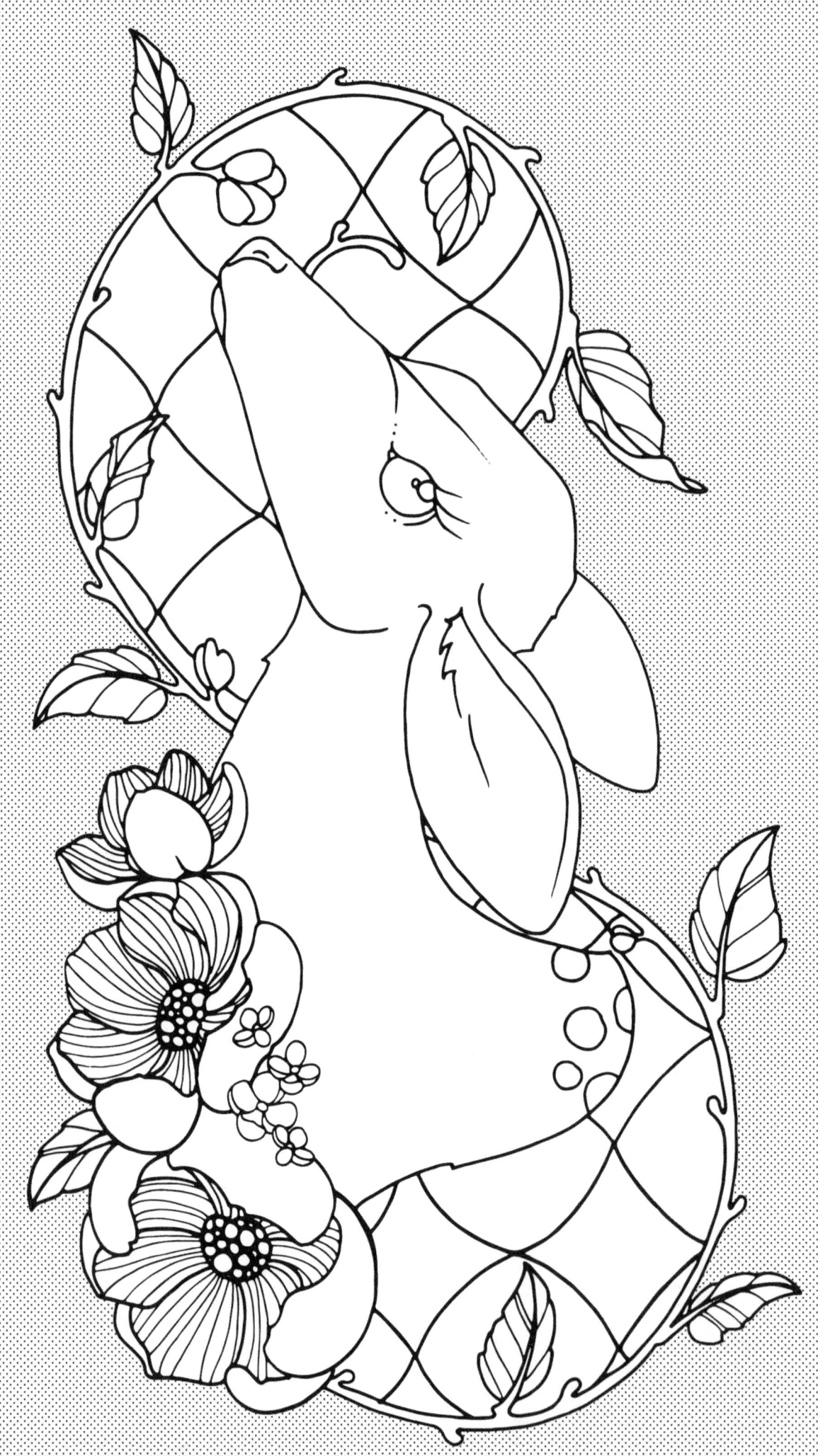

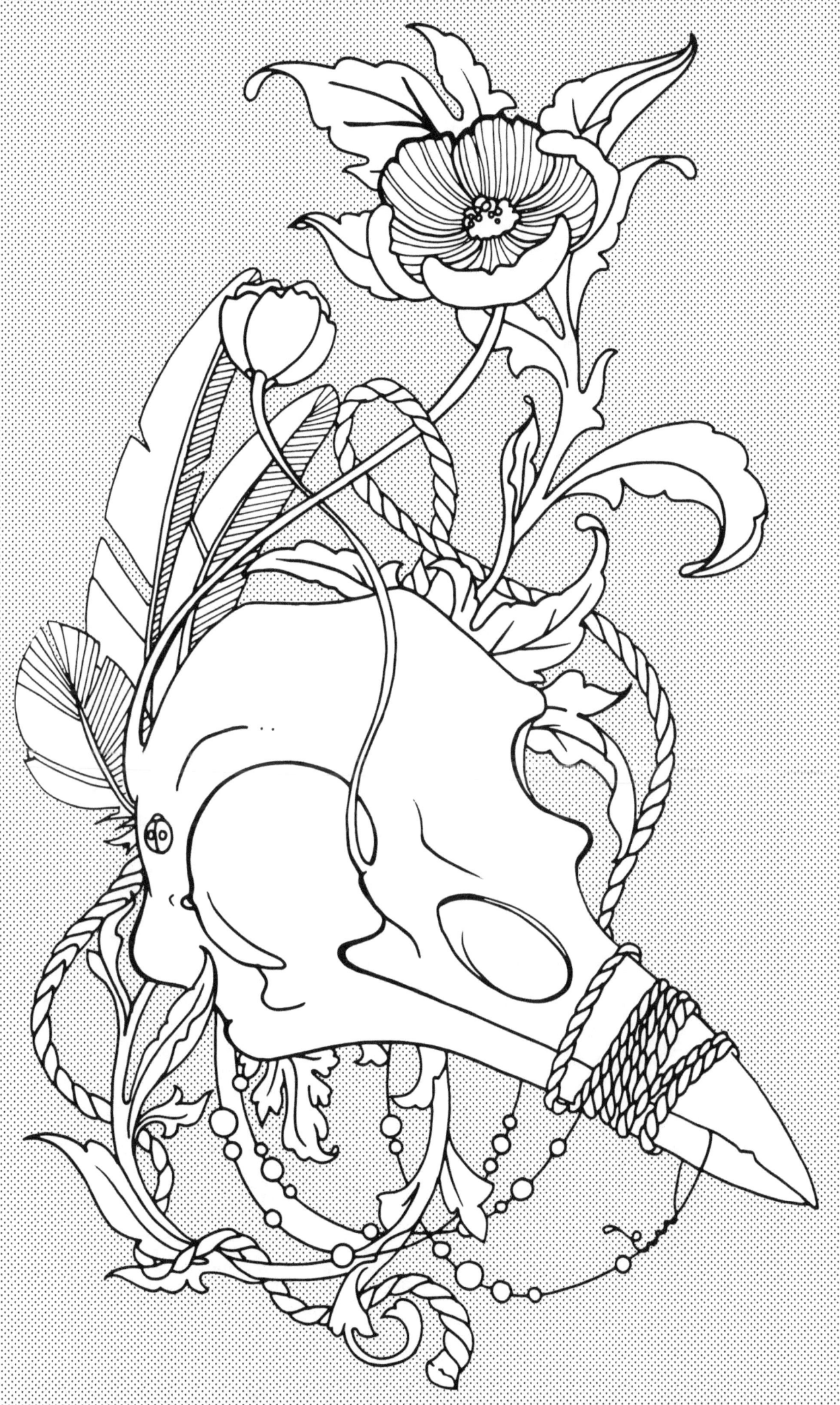

The Fox and The Crow

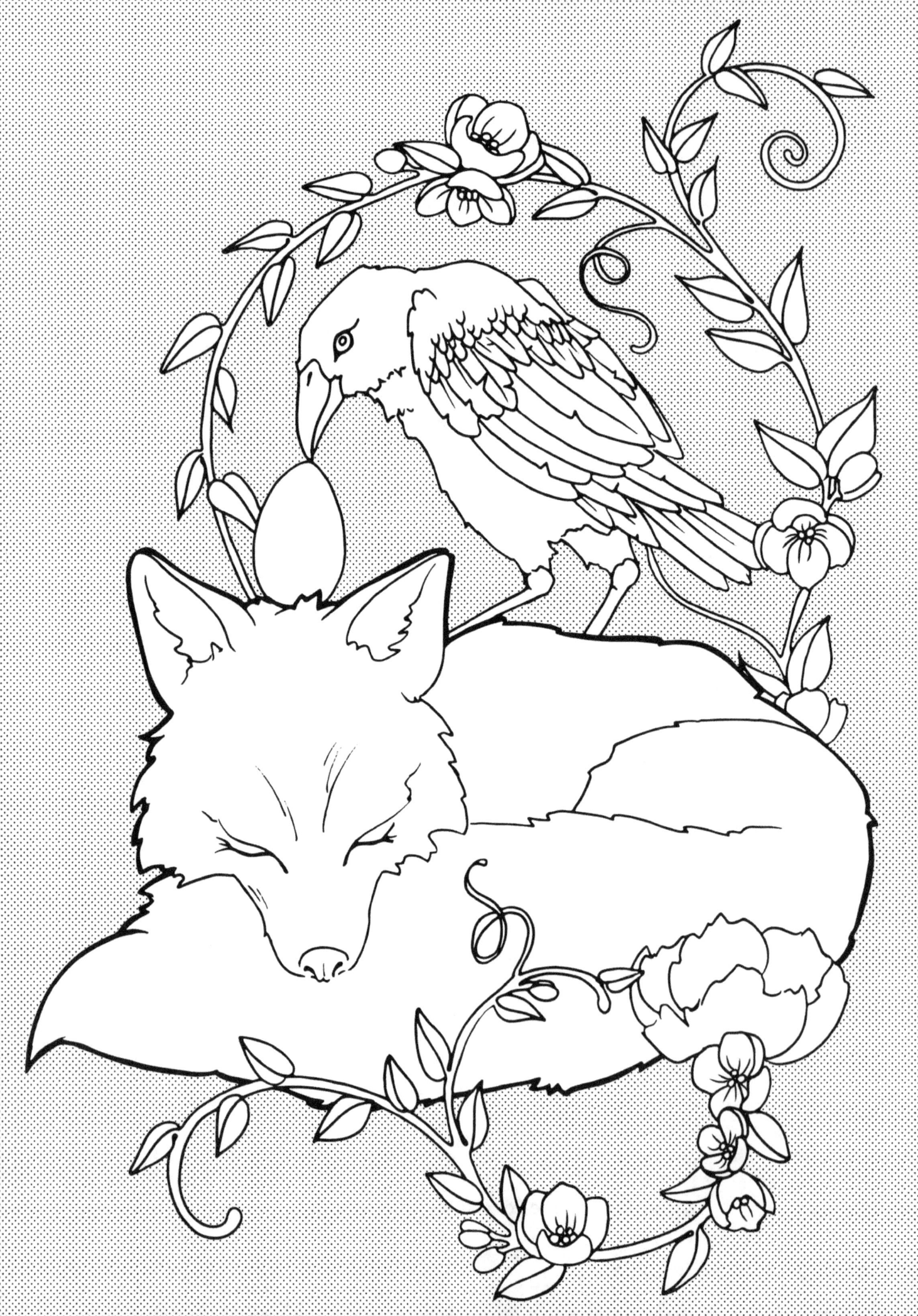

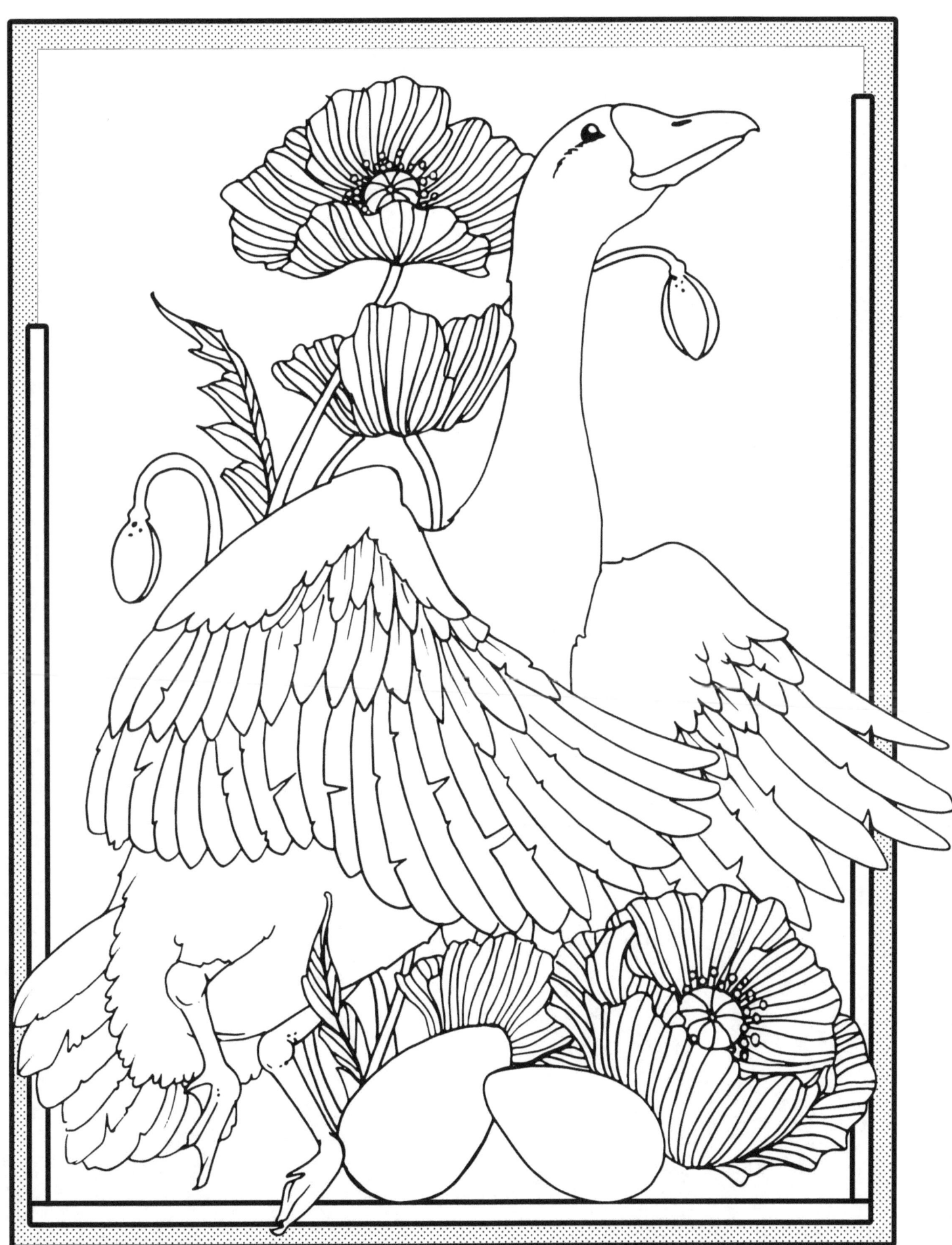

The Golden Goose

The Ice Queen

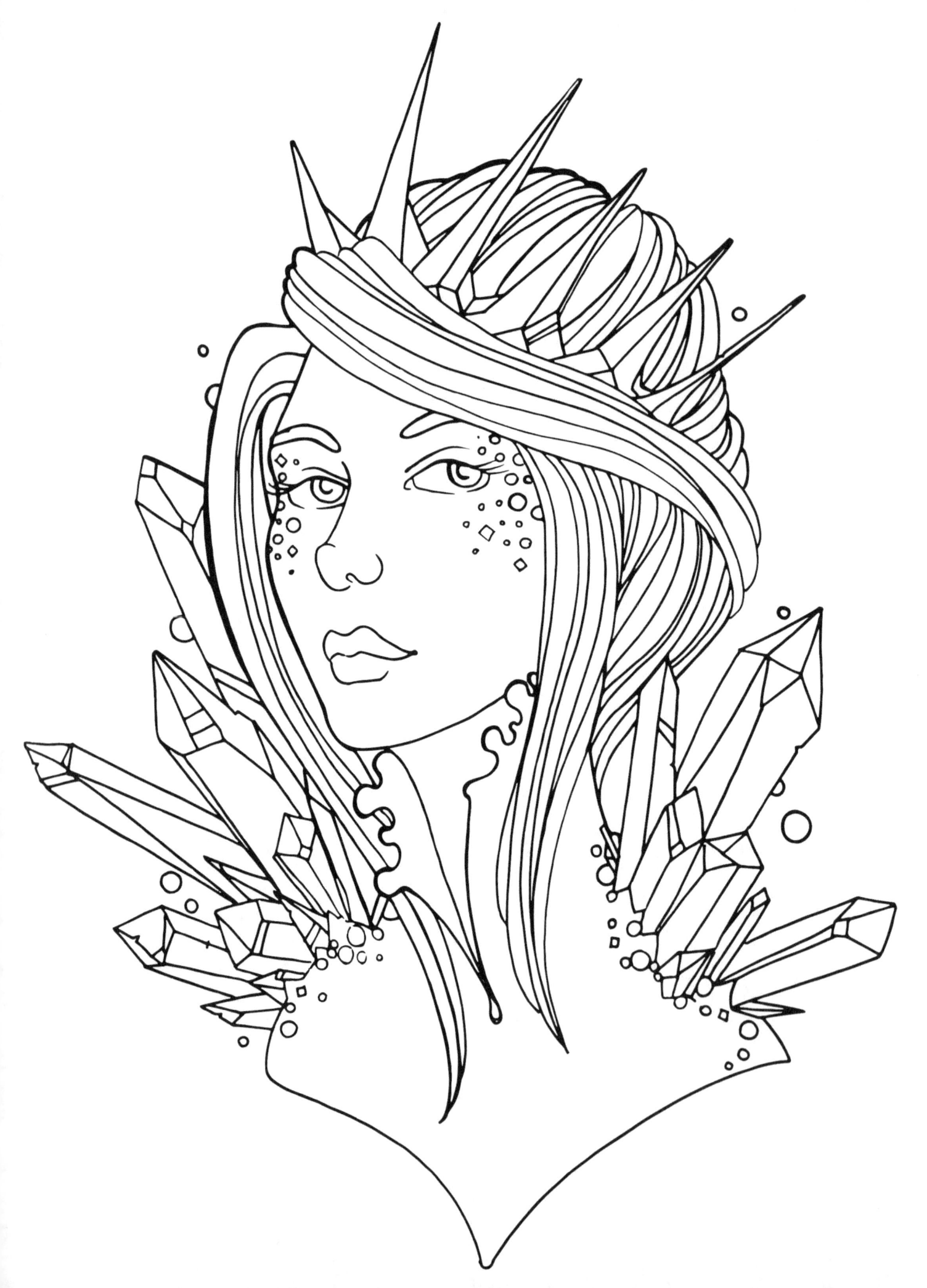

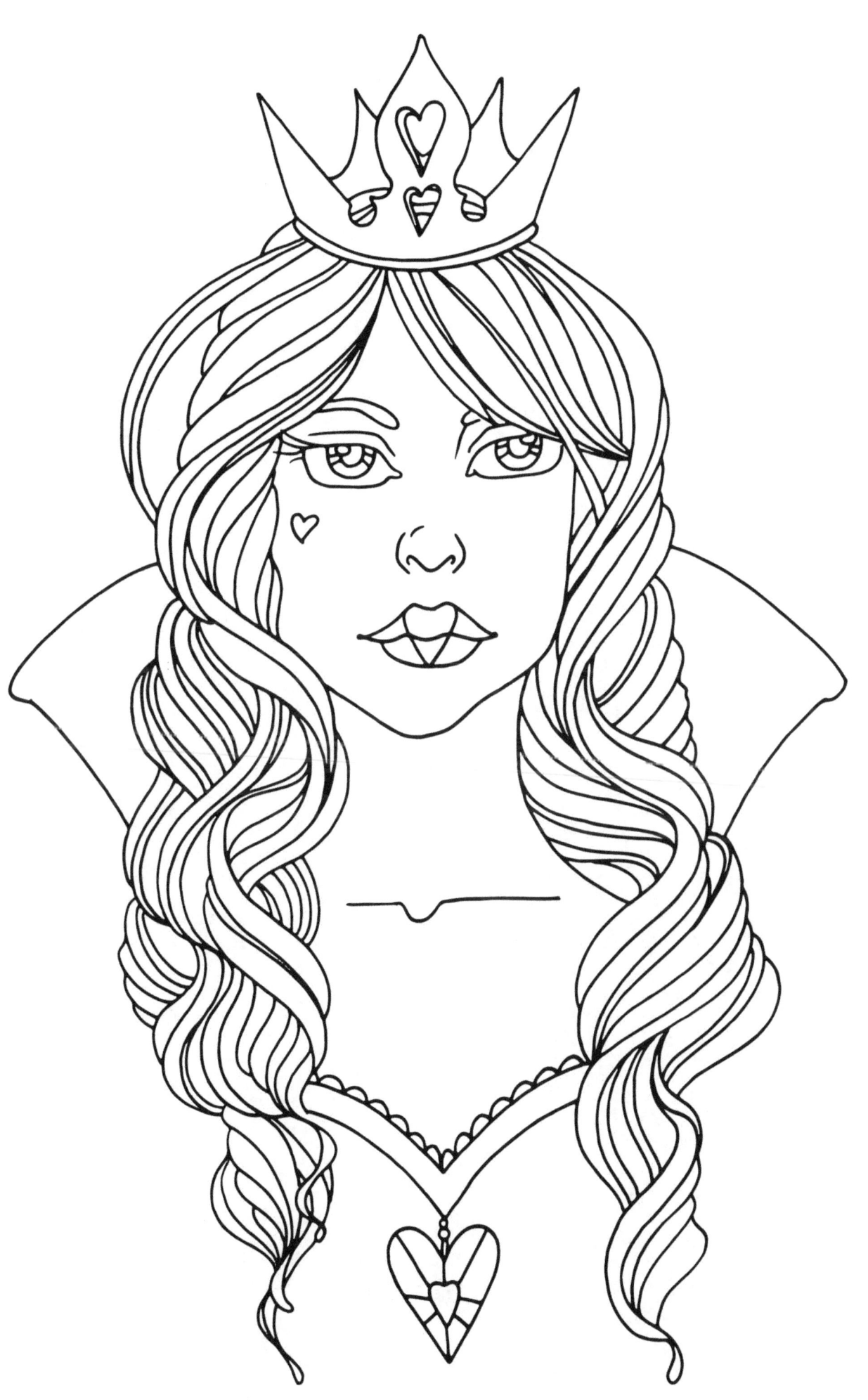

The Red Queen

Jack and the Beanstalk

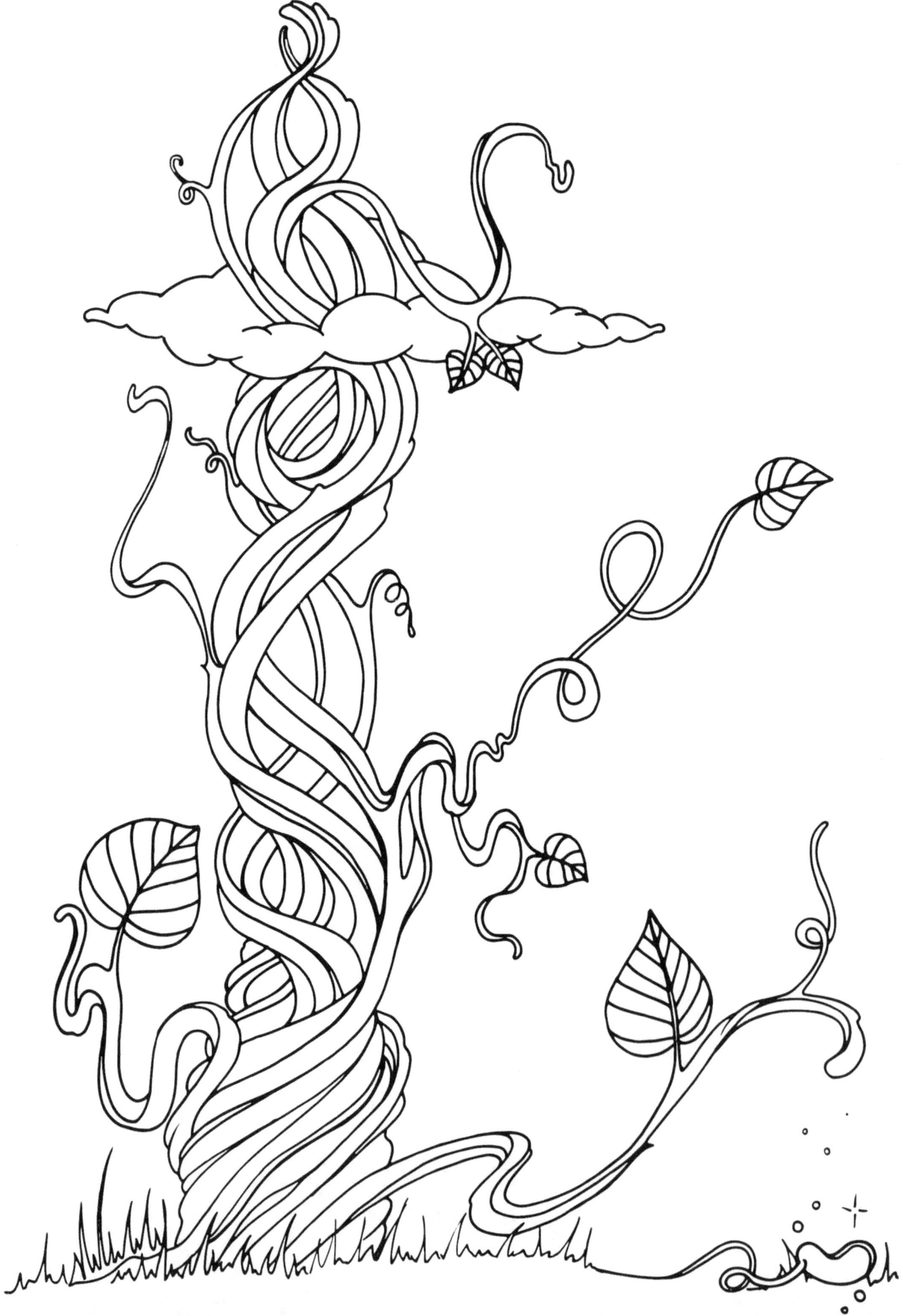

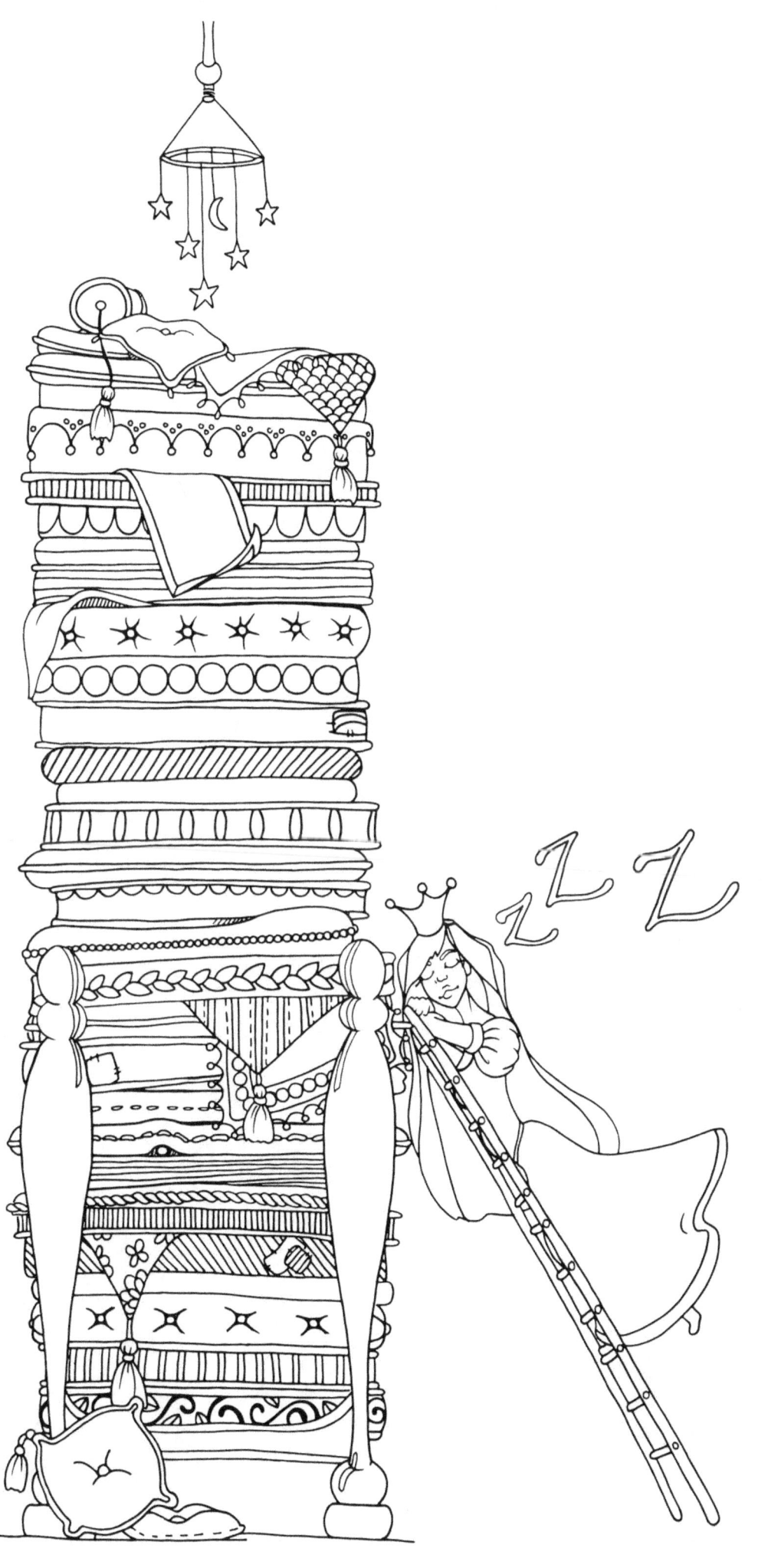

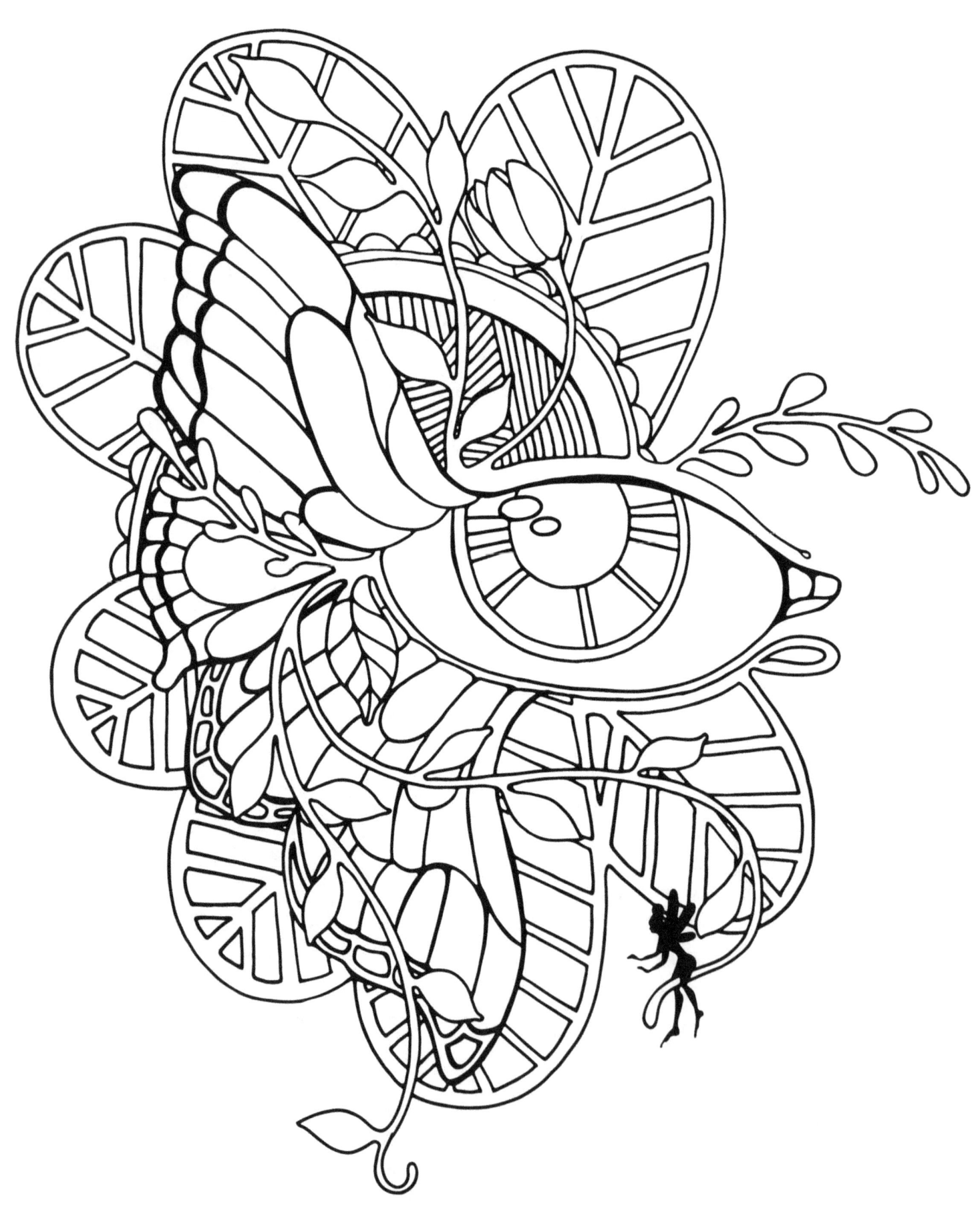

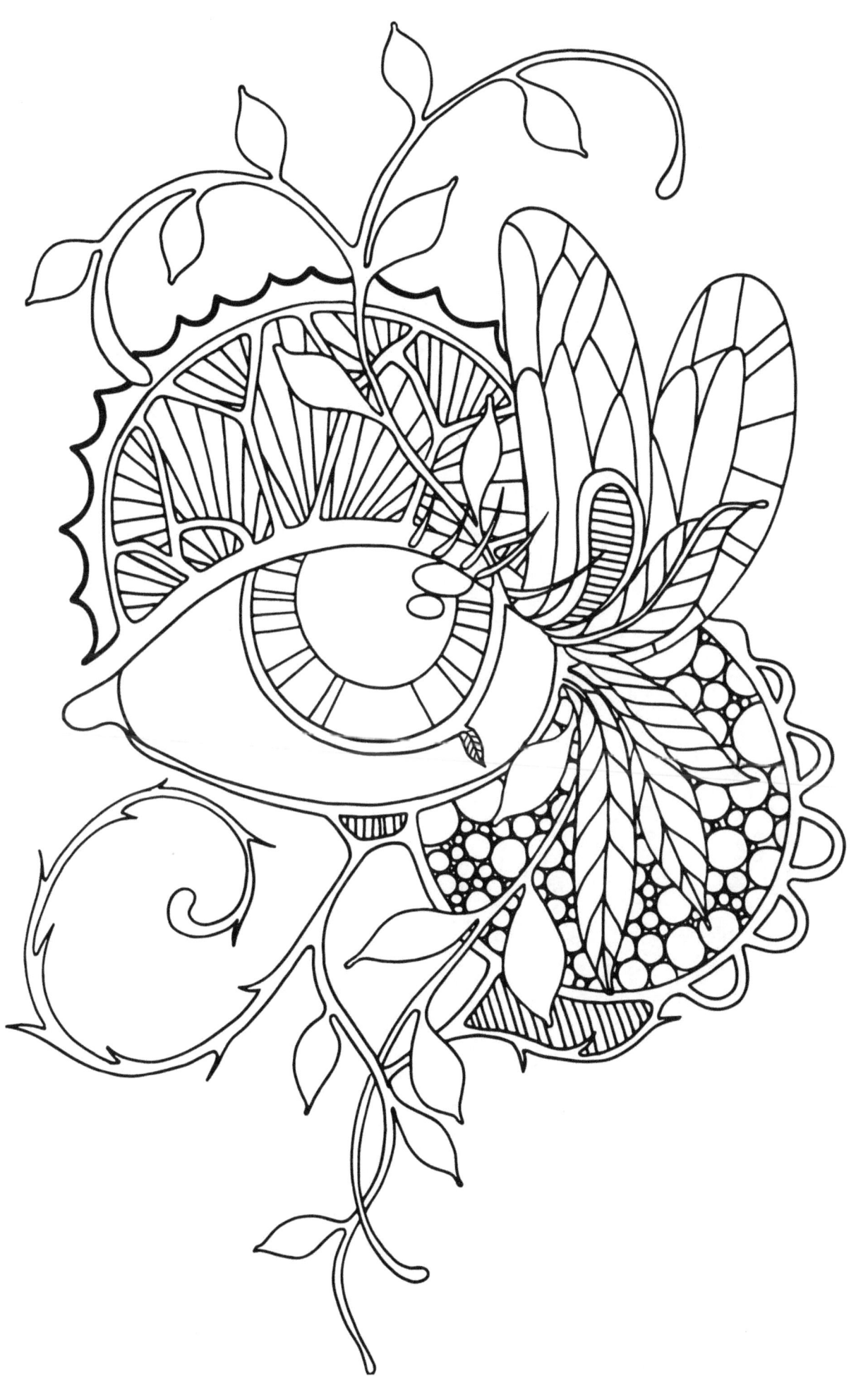

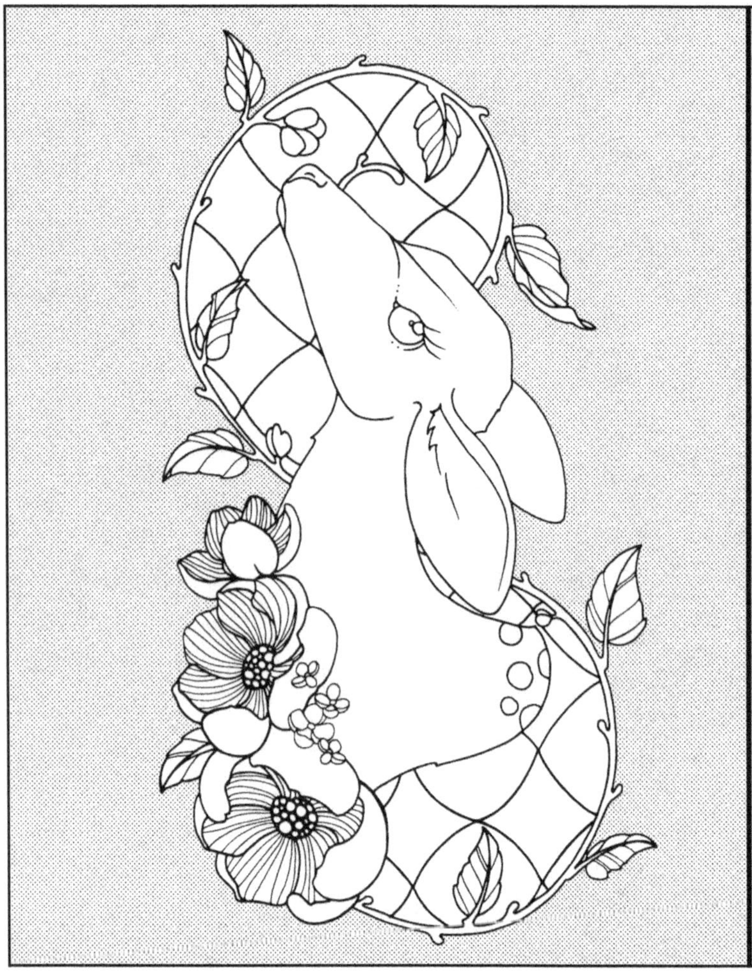
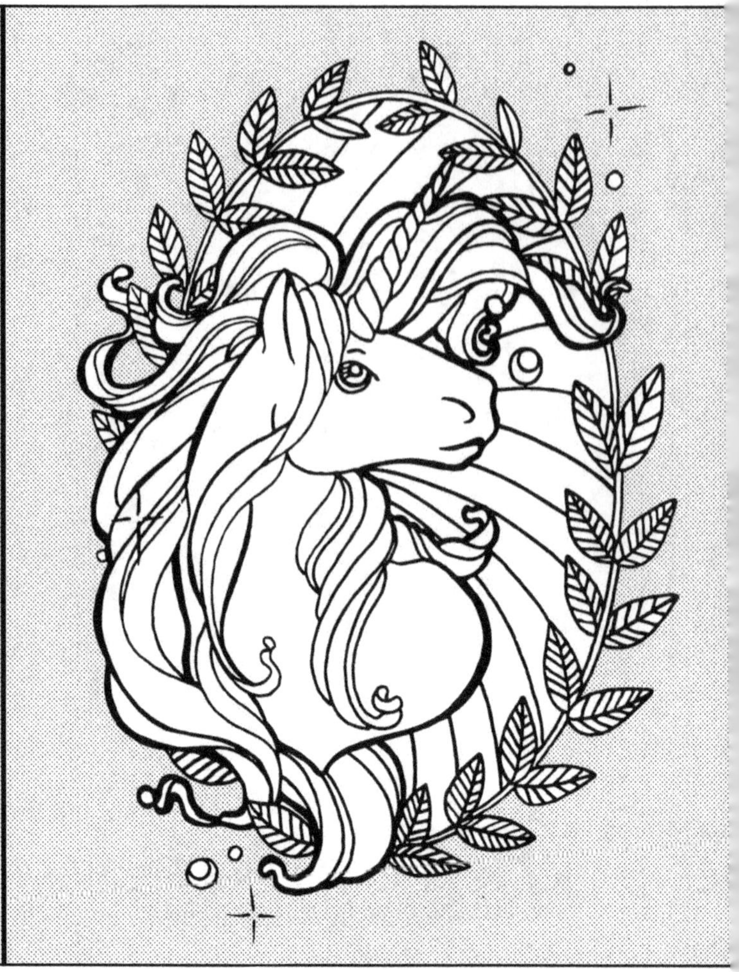
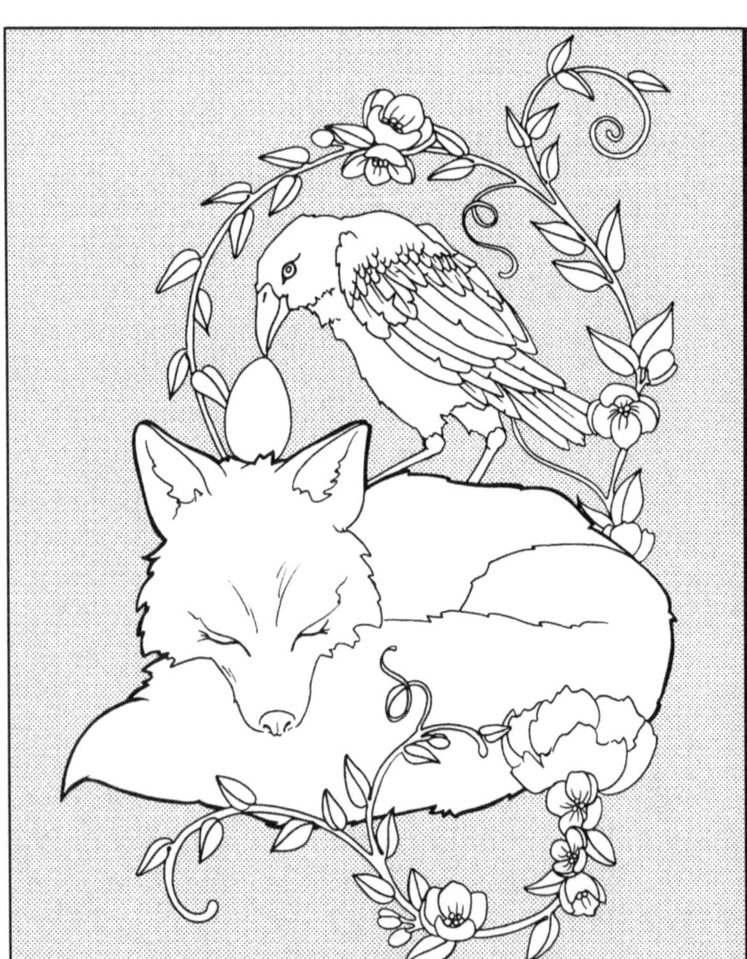
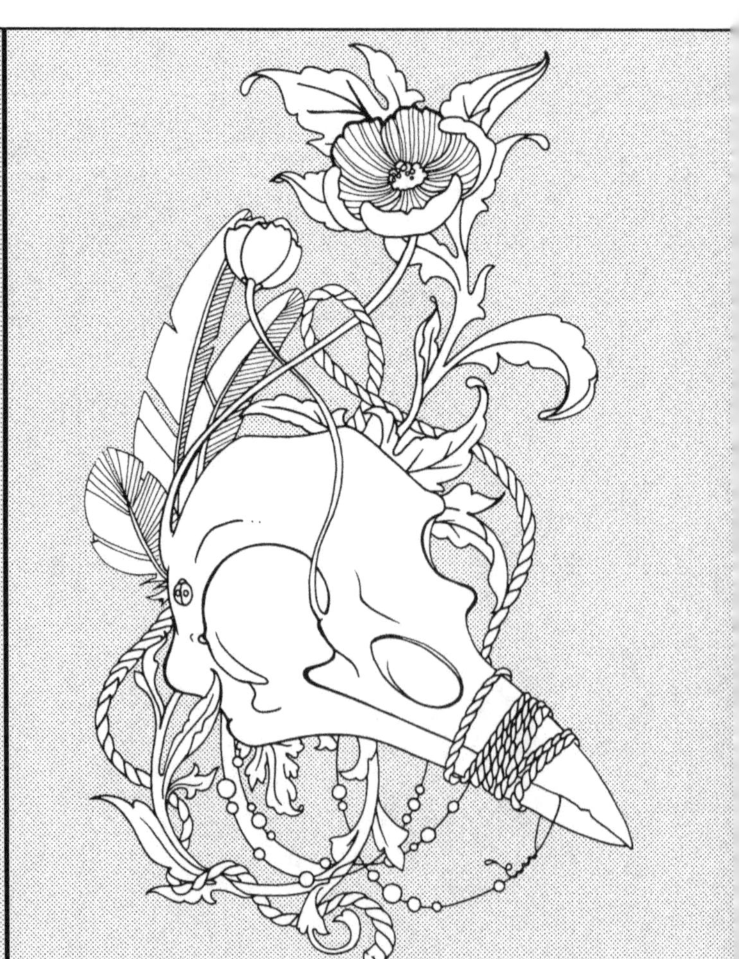

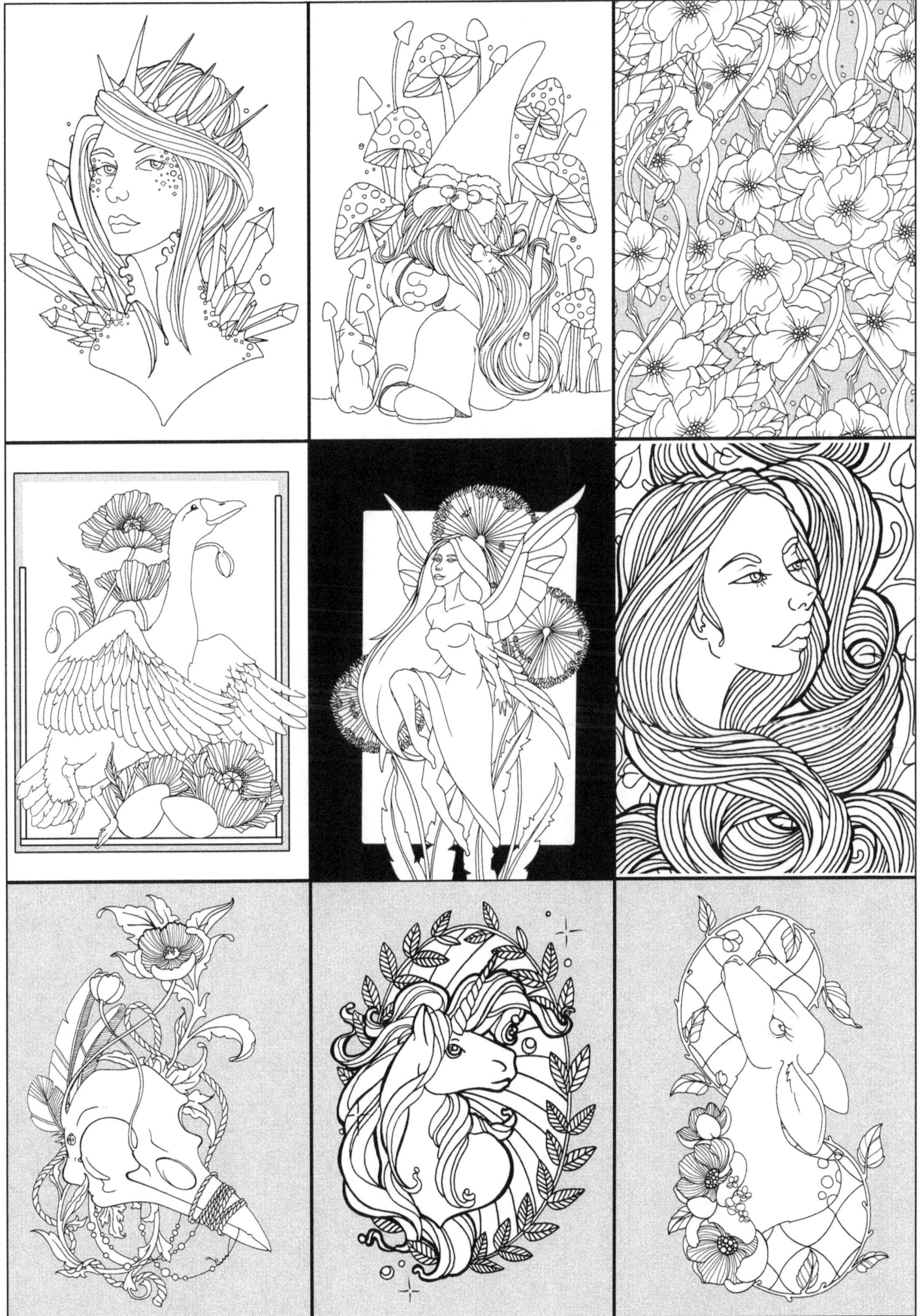

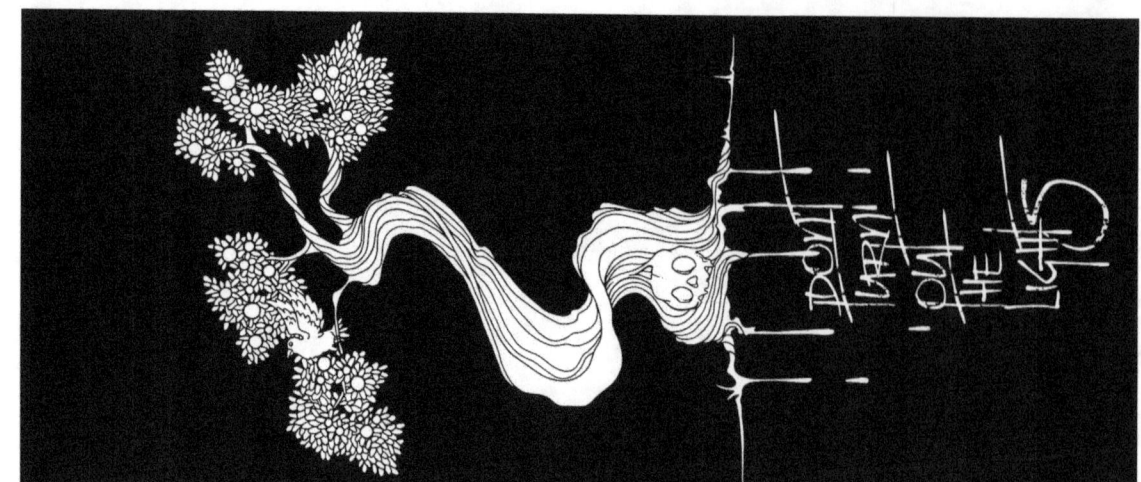

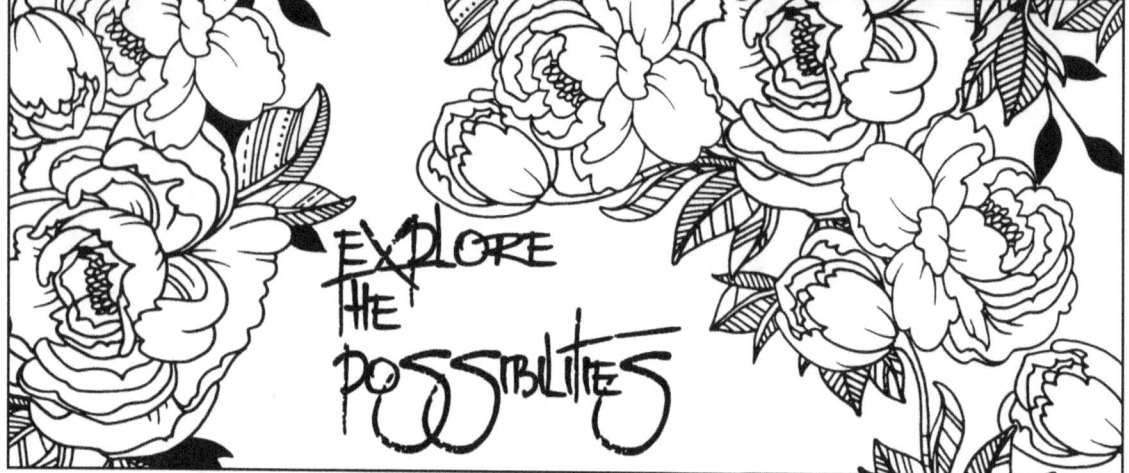

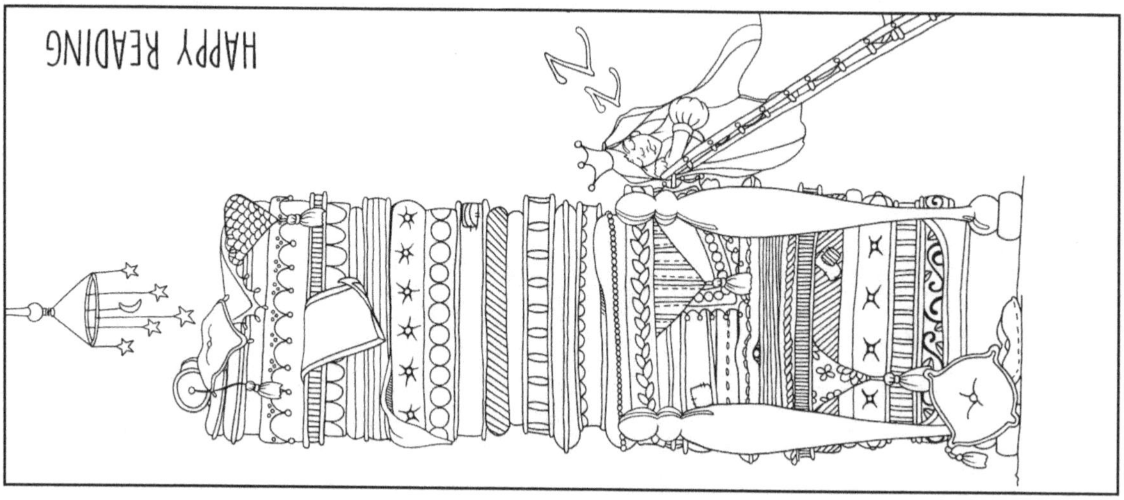

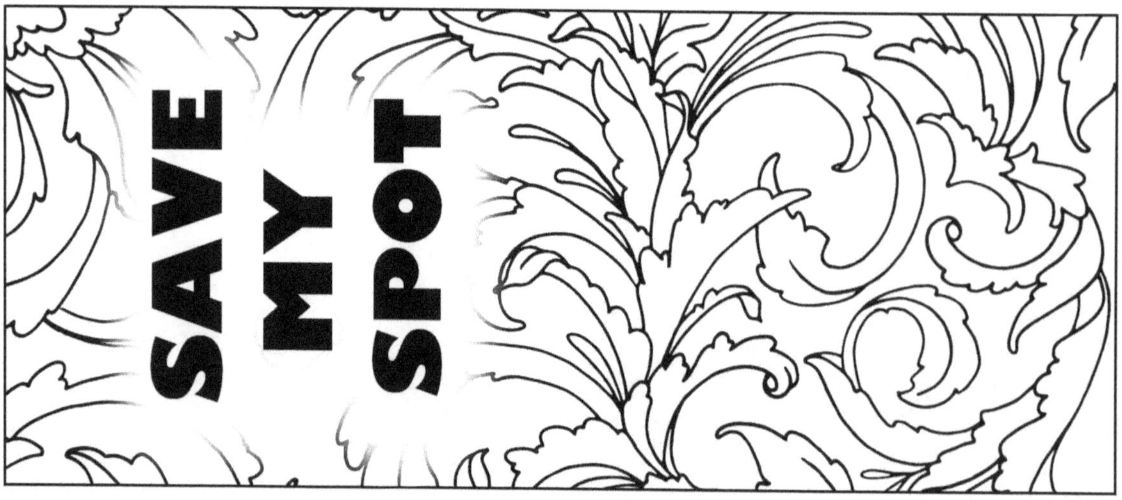

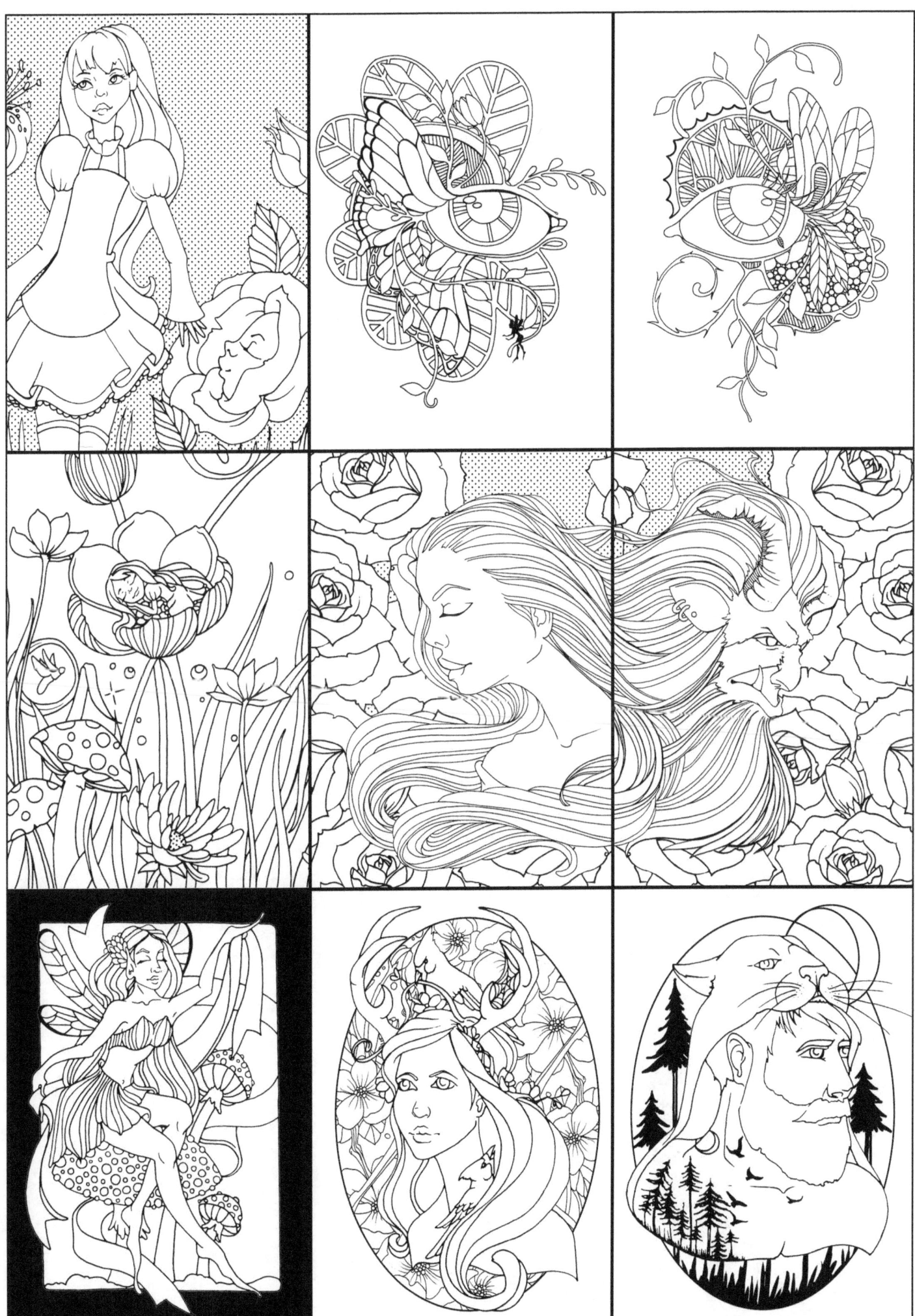

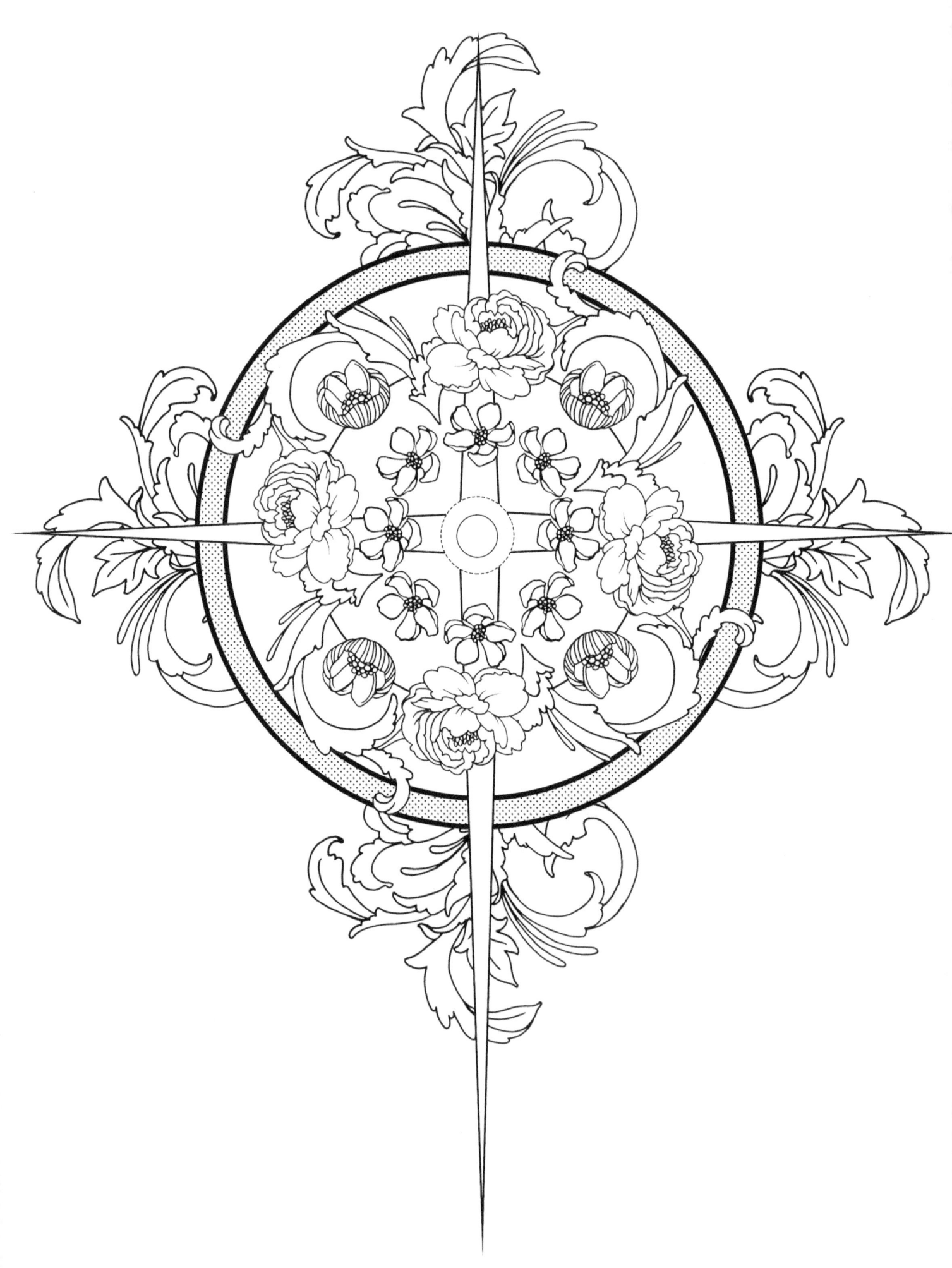

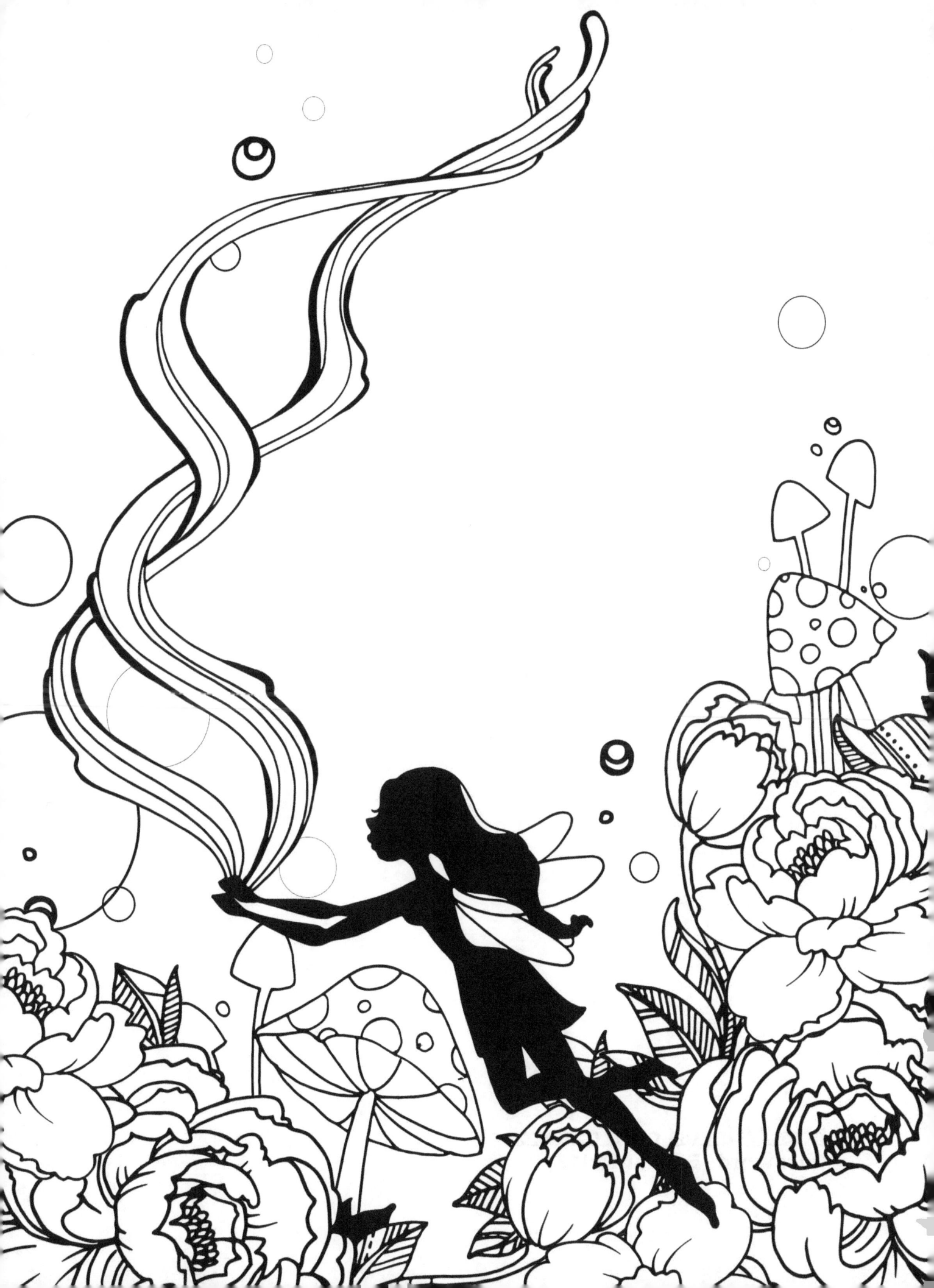

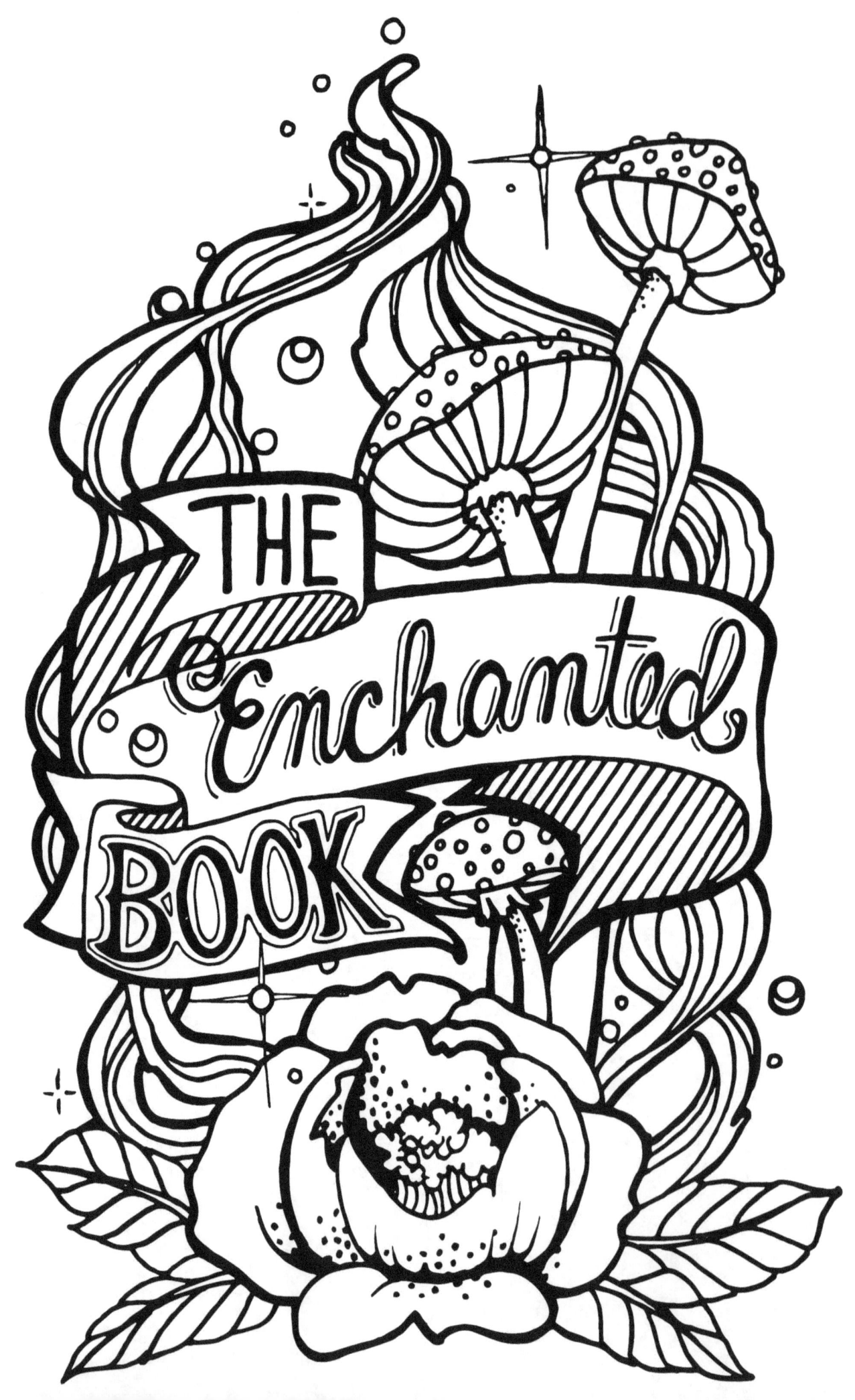

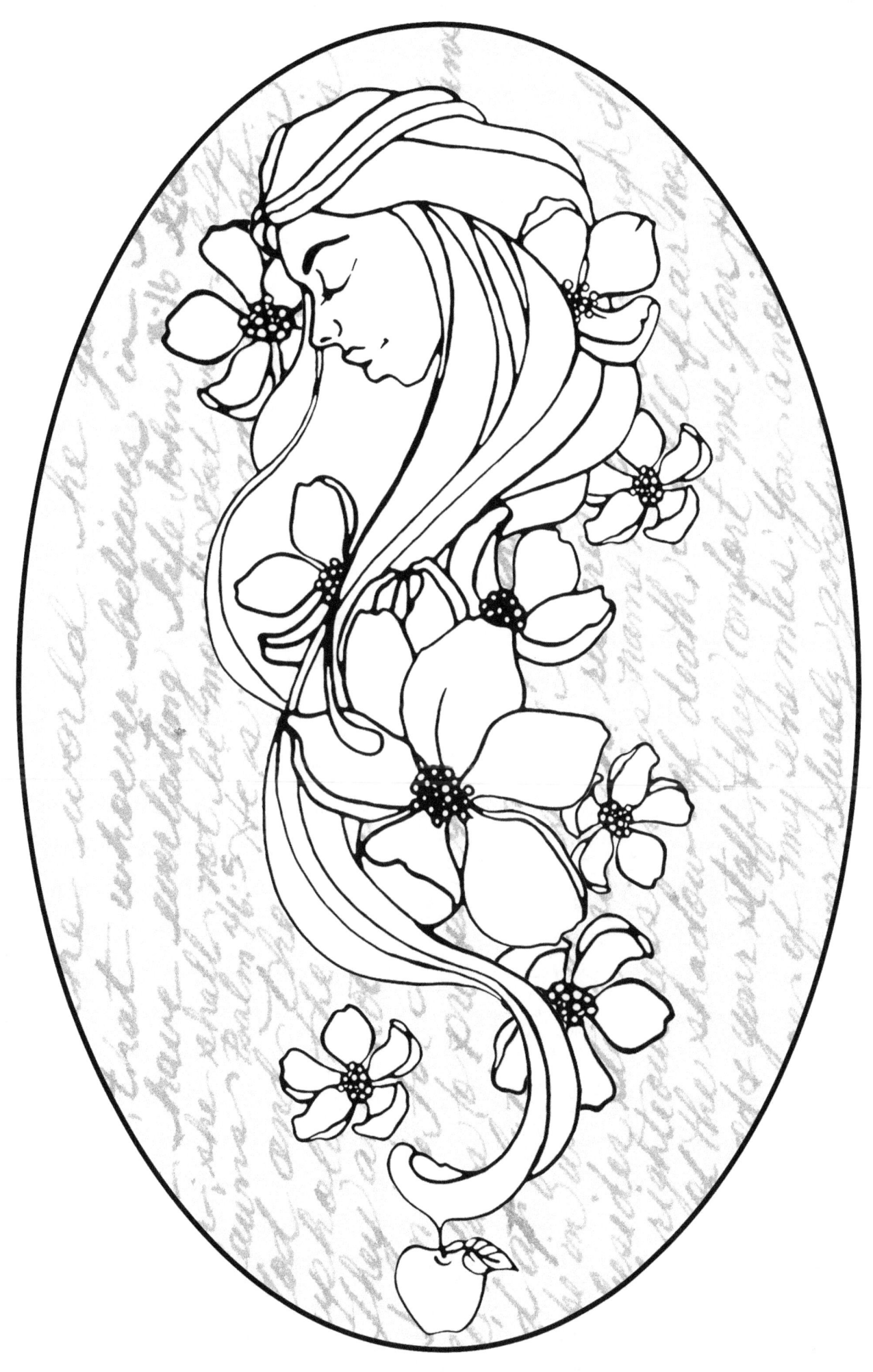

Preview from Creating In Faith, Color & Create Adult Coloring Book